THE MYSTERY AND WAYS OF DIVINE MERCY

Francis Kwaku Poku was educated in Ghana at O Poku Ware Secondary School, a Catholic boarding school. He then attended the University of Ghana and graduated with French with Latin as a subsidiary subject.

After university he worked in Ghana's security services and served in seven administrations. From 2001–2008 he was Ghana's National Security Co-ordinator and Cabinet Minister responsible for National Security. In 2006, he was awarded Ghana's most distinguished national honour, known as the Order of Volta, for his substantial contribution to peace and stability in Ghana and West Africa.

Francis is now resident in the UK where he is the chief executive of two UK companies, Africa Reconcile Limited and The Catholic Light Limited. He is a parishioner of the Church of Transfiguration in Kensal Rise, and was appointed by the Archdiocese of Westminster as chairman of the advisory board of the African Catholic Mission, a body responsible for co-ordinating the work of African chaplaincies in the UK. He is also the Catholic Church representative on the Ghana Christian Council in the UK.

He has been married for 42 years and has six children and nine grandchildren.

THE MYSTERY AND WAYS OF
Divine Mercy

FRANCIS KWAKU POKU

SilverWood

Published in 2013 by SilverWood Books
SilverWood Books
30 Queen Charlotte Street, Bristol, BS1 4HJ
www.silverwoodbooks.co.uk

ISBN 978-1-78132-090-7 (paperback)
ISBN 978-1-78132-094-5 (ebook)

British Library Cataloguing in Publication Data
A CIP catalogue record for this book is available from the British Library

Set in Bembo by SilverWood Books
Printed on responsibly sourced paper

*Oh Blessed Virgin Mary, You are the True Mother
even to those who do not know you.*

Pray for all your children.

*This book is dedicated to the memory of my parents, Joseph and Mary
Poku, whose lives were nothing but faith. Also to my dear wife, Isabella
Poku and children, Mary, Francis, Thomas, Elizabeth, Emmanuel
and Josephine who bore the pangs of my rather unsettled existence.*

Acknowledgements

I thank my daughter, Elizabeth, who moved from office to office with me as I struggled to combine consultancies and the writing of this book. My sincere gratitude also goes to the Association of Marian Helpers of Stockbridge, MA, the association in the church which is responsible for promoting the Divine Mercy devotions and who are also the copyright holders of the Diary of Saint Faustina. It granted us both the copyright and the permission to proceed to publish this book. For 8 months the representatives of the association undertook the review of the manuscript and made the necessary corrections. All the quotes in the book have been scrutinized by the association as appropriate for relevant use. I thank especially Megan Carlotta and Father Richard for their encouragement. My sincere thanks go to my publisher, especially Helen Hart, for their enthusiasm in helping us to complete the final processes related to publishing this book.

I wish to express my thanks to persons who were closest to me and who closely monitored the progress of this project. Among these persons are Jude Arthur, John OPoku Gyamfi, Matthew and Elizabeth Woahene; Douglas and Cornelia Darko, Irene Owusu-Ansah and Georgina Bempah.

Finally, I thank those who offered me the necessary spiritual support to enable me to write this book. These are Reverend Fathers Joseph Akono, B Isidore, Bernard Akoeso, Father Michael Mensah, Father Sean Thornton and the kindly parishioners of The Church of Transfiguration at Kensal Rise.

Contents

Author's Introduction

This book presents an unfolding spiritual journey, during which Christ appears to a Polish nun and directs her on the road to Christian perfection. In several encounters, which the nun was instructed to record in a diary, Christ uses her to remind us of the mysteries of our salvation, as recorded in the holy scripture. His main emphasis is what He describes as the greatest attribute of God, His merciful love for mankind.

In the encounters with Saint Faustina, God comes with great power to refocus our minds on the beginnings of our redemption. He redirects us from the vanities of this world, which lead to ruin, towards the Heart of Jesus, from which graces flow to redeem humanity. Through Saint Faustina, Christ evokes for us visions of His suffering on the cross, of heaven, hell and purgatory as well as the fundamental truths revealed in the scripture. By responding faithfully to Christ's call, Saint Faustina has become a true revelation of God's mercy and through her Christ calls us to undertake new devotions and make sacrifices for our redemption.

The mystical experience of Saint Faustina is in some ways a re-enactment of the experiences of the prophets of the Old Testament. She is set apart by God and directed by grace to endure all manner of physical and interior suffering and trials to accomplish God's merciful designs for the world. She unites herself with God's will and becomes a martyr of love for God and neighbour. Throughout her consecrated life, precisely because of her perfect charity, she accepts with gladness all her trials, humiliations and frustrations and she accomplishes God's designs of mercy for souls.

The Divine Mercy message and devotions that were entrusted to Saint Faustina were intended for the whole of humanity. Her missionary role is the same as that of the prophets of Israel, when their people forgot about what God had done for them and started to live as if there were no God. In a similar way, Christ now comes to reaffirm through Saint Faustina that God His Father created us in love and that even when we sinned, He did not abandon us. He showed us great mercy and put in place mysterious designs to bring us back to Himself. Through His only begotten Son, Our Lord Jesus Christ, God continues to distribute graces to sinful humanity.

Designs of God's Mercy: Life According to the Spirit

From the time that Christ called Saint Faustina to fulfil God's purpose, the essential message that comes to light is that in submitting to God's will, the soul must live according to the spirit. The soul lives in the flesh but to be able to gain an insight into the mysteries and ways of God, it must submit to God's will. By acknowledging God's invisible presence in us and obeying His commandments, we are transformed to become His adopted children in Christ. Moses explained the relationship as follows: "For us right living will mean this: To keep and observe all these commandments before the Lord Our God as He has directed us." (Deut: 6:4–25)

In the new kingdom, the soul must believe that through Christ, God has bestowed on humanity His merciful gifts of the spirit and, if the soul responds to these gifts, He advances towards perfection in Christ. All of God's commandments and revelations point humanity to life according to the spirit, which brings true life in God, because life according to the flesh leads to confusion of the mind, darkness and death. Christ showed us an example by living according to the spirit and forsaking the world unto the cross, in obedience to His Father. Since Christ lived by the spirit, all the visible actions and the events of His life have become for us saving events that wrought our salvation. The life of Christ is therefore a manifestation of Divine Mercy because His life glorified God His Father and by His sacrifice He redeems humanity. All faithful souls are called upon to imitate Christ by living this mystery of Divine Mercy. It is summarised neatly for us by Saint Maximus the Confessor: "The Word of God, born once on the level of the flesh, is always born willingly for those who desire it on the level of the spirit because of His love for men."

Distribution of Divine Mercy to Mankind

It is an affirmation of our faith that it was through Christ that all things were created. In his own mystery, God uses His Trinitarian nature to restore humanity to Himself.

The Trinitarian rescue of humanity was effected by the will of the Father, who sent His only begotten Son to redeem mankind. In that mystery, the Blessed Virgin Mary conceived by the Holy Spirit. It is the greatest act of mercy because Christ, even though He was God, emptied Himself of His glory and took our human nature to redeem mankind. Through the incarnation of Christ and His earthly sacrifices, humanity is united with God our Creator. Christ has become the light of the world and the measure of our true human existence.

The Sacraments and Divine Mercy

In the mystery of God's mercy, Christ continues the work of salvation through the sacraments. This presence is empowered by the Holy Spirit because God the Father pours out his graces only in Christ. Also by the sacraments, Christ makes Himself available to every faithful person individually and by the gifts of the Spirit guides him to his true end in God. By the sacraments, Christ builds a faith community which shares the graces of his paschal mystery. Divine mystery is therefore offered to all in Christ by the will of the Father who distributes gifts through the Holy Spirit.

Trust and Divine Mercy

In His encounter with Saint Faustina, Christ emphasises the fundamental importance of trust for the efficacious distribution of Divine Mercy. Trust enables souls to receive the gifts occasioned by the various devotions to Divine Mercy.

On the question of trust, Saint Augustine instructs us that God has planted His Spirit in us which naturally guides us to Him. Another saint, Hippolytus, explains that our faith, which is the foundation of our trust, is not blind and that our faith is based on what God the Father communicated to mankind through Christ; that it was Christ as the Word of God who revealed mysteries to us through the prophets until the Word became flesh. He revealed to mankind the truth and ways of God. Hippolytus said Christ revealed suffering in His own life so as also to reveal His glory through resurrection. The saint summarises it as follows: "We do not put our faith in empty phrases, we are not carried off by sudden impulses of the heart, we are not seduced by plausible and eloquent speech; but we do not refuse belief to words spoken by Divine Power."

Indeed our trust is based on the continuous revelation of God's power and majesty; throughout salvation history, God has been shown as faithful to his promises. He fulfilled His promise to send the Messiah and through miracles and signs, He has confirmed the existence of a spiritual system that surpasses the natural order. We can also see in His justice that all His commandments and revealed attributes are for the good of humanity. In Christ he reveals His compassion for Man and becomes for us a model of perfect human life. Also, by the merits of Christ, God forgives us and bestows on us the gifts of His Spirit to begin our eternal life, even in this world.

The Fruits of Trust

Trust in God's mercy therefore effects in us the revelation of the indwelling gifts of grace and leads us to understand the active presence of God in our lives. It promotes a deeper understanding of His ways and familiarity with the Living Christ. Trust also strengthens us to be prepared to share in Christ's earthly sacrifice and makes us better able to overcome our spiritual enemies. As our minds become illuminated through trust, we gain better understanding of God's mysteries and ways. Through trust, we develop confidence in God's mercy through remorse, contrition and a firm purpose of amendment. Through the disposition of trust, we gain the graces necessary to do good works.

Divine Mercy: The Blessed Virgin Mary and Faithful Souls

The Blessed Virgin Mary has always been a faithful mother and guide of all souls seeking perfection in her Son, Our Lord Jesus Christ. Therefore, in the manifestation of Divine Mercy through

Saint Faustina, a special place of honour is assigned to the Blessed Virgin Mary. Considerable attention has been assigned to this theme to enable faithful souls to understand the place of the Blessed Virgin Mary in the history of our redemption. Her role has been manifested before, during and after Christ. She continues to guide souls in the way of redemption and has been referred to as God's "Glory and Splendour".

Human and Spiritual arguments have been advanced to explain her role in God's plan of redemption. On the human level, we appreciate that during great human wars, special honours, including medals, are awarded to those who distinguish themselves. As Christ discloses to Saint Faustina that we are engaged in spiritual warfare against the principalities of evil, does it not make sense that the Blessed Virgin Mary, who has played a pivotal role in the war against Satan, should be assigned a place of honour by God? During Christ's earthly life, it was the Virgin Mary who acted as a faithful mother during all the difficult events of His birth, life and death. She was present with the apostles, even after the resurrection, to give them support and was with them during the coming of the Holy Spirit.

On the spiritual level, it was to her that God announced the mystery of Christ's birth by the Holy Spirit. She was also specially prepared for Christ's birth by her own Immaculate Conception (the mystery of her own birth without sin). This mystery was confirmed by her during her apparition at Lourdes. She was present at the foot of the cross when Christ's body was offered as a sacrifice to His Father. Our Lady was our human representative during the sacrifice and the whole of humanity was entrusted to Her by Christ. In the mystery of our redemption, Our Lady becomes our mother and guide who leads the whole of humanity to participate in the redemptive work of Christ. Mary was therefore not only the greatest beneficiary of God's mercy in this world but even from heaven, she continues to show her love and mercy for her suffering children. It has been established in the present work that throughout history, she has been present in the spiritual life of the Church through signs and miracles, and that most of the saints who have performed heroic works for Christ have been devoted to her. She is the perfect reflection of God's mercy.

Saint Faustina and Divine Mercy

Saint Faustina showed herself to be a perfect candidate for her apostolate of mercy. As a child, she was physically weak, suffering from tuberculosis till the end of her short life of thirty-three years. She was virtually illiterate, with only three years of education, leaving home at the age of fourteen to earn a living as a domestic.

However, this was the girl who was chosen by Christ to imitate His sacrifice and to become the apostle of the Divine Mercy message. She suffered a lot through prayer, fasting and exposure to ridicule and contempt. She was nevertheless able to communicate Christ's message through exalted thoughts and clear insights into the mysteries of God. In her, Christ showed the power of the weak and of suffering.

During one of her encounters with Christ, He revealed to her that there would be a time when her work as the apostle of Divine Mercy would be rejected, but that God would act with great power to give evidence of the message's authenticity. Indeed, in 1959, the Vatican suppressed the messages but the ban was lifted in 1978 by Pope John Paul II, who was from her native Poland and had been a great supporter of her messages. Her sanctity was affirmed by a miracle that led to her beatification. Maureen Digan of the United States was praying at the tomb of Saint Faustina when she heard a voice saying "Ask for my help and I will help you." The lady was suffering from lymphedema, a disease which causes large swellings due to fluid retention. Two days after hearing that voice, the fluid retention stopped. Five doctors testified that there was no scientific explanation for her healing. After investigation, the Vatican declared the healing miraculous. Faustina was canonised and became the first saint of the twenty-first century.

The present work has been undertaken to promote a deeper understanding of Saint Faustina's apostleship of Divine Mercy, her heroic sacrifice for the glory of God and the salvation of souls. It has been emphasised that all her revelations have been shown to be consistent with the scripture and traditions of the Church. Because she was transformed into God's mercy, she in turn reflects God's mercy to other souls. In so doing, she empties herself of all human pleasures and passions to unite her will with God's will.

Her message has been described in the diaries as an urgent reminder to a world of people distracted by the search for material goods and plagued by doubts about their destination. Christ comes with mercy through the saint to remind the world that the scriptures are there to give us hope. Christ revealed to her that a sign of the cross will appear in the sky just before the final judgement. The message to Saint Faustina must therefore be seen as urgent. All faithful Christians are called upon to embrace the Divine Mercy message with true devotion and trust.

The Devotions

Through Saint Faustina, Christ came to establish new forms of devotion to the Divine Mercy. These have been quoted in the book. The five devotions are:

1   The Image of the Merciful Jesus to Saint Faustina with the signature "Jesus, I Trust in You." Christ promised eternal salvation, great progress in the way of Christian perfection, the grace of a happy death and all other possible graces which people will ask of Him with trust.

2   Feast of Divine Mercy – To be celebrated on the Sunday after Easter. There are extraordinary promises attached to the celebration of the feast, including the complete remission of sins and punishment.

3   Chaplet of the Divine Mercy – This is a prayer of atonement and for the appeasement of God's anger, by offering to God the Body and Blood, Soul and Divinity of Jesus Christ.

4   The Hour of Mercy – To be honoured each day. This is a prayer of appeal to Jesus and to the value and merits of Christ's passion. Christ explained that during this hour, the faithful can obtain for themselves and for others great favours.

5   The Novena – A novena to the Divine Mercy to begin on Good Friday as a preparation for the feast.

The Importance of the Devotions

The devotions lead us to reflect on the truths of our salvation as contained in the scriptures. They must be considered as spiritual exercises which promote spiritual growth. They help the faithful to develop a strong bond between themselves and God the Creator, enabling them to enjoy the inward presence of God in themselves. They strengthen us to unite our will with God's will. The devotions help us to bear our trials and sufferings and therefore overcome the world, the Devil and the flesh. Also, remembering that Christ reveals that in this world we are engaged in spiritual warfare, the prayers and works of devotion enkindle in us the spiritual dispositions that we need to face evil days. We remember most importantly that the Divine Mercy devotions have the blessing of God the Father, who offers us graces through the merits of Our Lord Jesus Christ.

This book has added "Great Devotions" which originate from Christ's redemptive work. These devotions are the Sacred Heart, the Heart from which flows the streams of God's mercy and devotions to the great family of the incarnation, The Blessed Virgin Mary and Saint Joseph. As God is blessed in His angels and in His saints, we give a special place of honour to Saint Michael and the angels who have been eternally faithful to God.

May the name of the Almighty God, who continues to guide and guard creation, be blessed now and forever more. Amen.

PART 1

Sources of Divine Mercy

CHAPTER 1

The Call to God's Service

Saint Faustina begins her diary by recounting the dramatic events that led to her call by Christ to consecrate her life to God and later to become an apostle of Divine Mercy. The saint recalls that, at the age of seven, she heard God's voice in her soul calling her to a more perfect life but had no one to instruct her. When Saint Faustina was eighteen, a strange encounter with Christ occurred which would alter her whole existence.

The saint had asked her parents' permission to enter the convent but they had refused. She therefore decided to forget about any religious call and started to take refuge in social activities. She was at a dance with her sister when she saw a vision which she describes as follows: "As I began to dance, I suddenly saw Jesus at my side, Jesus racked with pain, stripped of His clothing, all covered with wounds, who spoke these words to me: **'How long shall I put up with you and how long will you keep putting Me off?'** At that moment the charming music stopped, and the company I was with vanished from my sight; there remained Jesus and I." (Diary 9)

According to the account given by the saint in her diary, she left the dance and went to the Cathedral of Stanislaus Kostka, where she prostrated herself before the Blessed Sacrament, begging the Lord for an understanding as to what she should do next. An interior voice directed her to go to a convent in Warsaw. Saint Faustina then went home, packed all her things and left for Warsaw, only confiding in her sister what had happened. Not knowing what to do, once in Warsaw, she prayed to the Virgin Mary for help and was directed by a voice to a safe lodging for the night. Through a series of struggles, she was at last accepted in a convent. She expressed her spiritual satisfaction as follows: "God filled my soul with the interior light of a deeper knowledge of Him as Supreme Goodness and Supreme Beauty. I came to know very much God loves me." (Diary 16)

However, as Saint Faustina acquired a deeper knowledge of God's goodness and beauty, and as she became committed to prayer, she became disillusioned by the worldliness around her. She began to observe that there was little time for prayer and, also, that there was general laxity and indiscipline. She was on the point of going to announce her departure from the convent when she saw Jesus. She narrates as follows in her diary: "After a while brightness filled my cell, and on the curtain I saw the very sorrowful Face of Jesus. There were open wounds on His Face, and large tears were falling on my bedspread. Not knowing what all this meant I asked Jesus, "Jesus, who has hurt You so?" And Jesus said to me: **'It is you who will cause me this pain if you leave this convent. It is to this place that I called you and nowhere else; and I have prepared many graces for you.'** (Diary 19)

The saint quickly submitted to the will of her Saviour and made her confession at the next opportunity. Not long after the crisis, our Lord permitted her guardian angel to take the saint to see purgatory.

Call, a Gift of Divine Mercy

In an act of God's mercy, originating from His great love for humanity, He calls us through His Son, our Lord Jesus Christ, to make deeds and sacrifices that will transform us and make it possible for us to share in the divinity of Christ. Thus God is not only rescuing us, by His calls, from eternal death; by His invitation He intends to confer on us a glory greater than we had before the fall of Adam. Therefore, whenever God calls us to fulfil His purpose, He is in effect calling us to perfection and eternal glory.

Thus it was that when, through God's messenger Gabriel, God called the Virgin Mary to help accomplish His plan of salvation, she saw it as God's merciful action and, inspired by the Holy Spirit, foresaw that she had been called to glory and that, indeed, all generations would call her blessed. To the Blessed Virgin, the cost of fulfilling God's mission did not count, so overwhelming was the power of the caller (God) and the importance of the mission: humanity's salvation.

Special Graces accompany every Call to God's Service

In His mercy, God gives interior gifts of grace to all souls in the measure that the gifts are necessary to accomplish His purposes. When bestowed, these graces raise the soul to a greater understanding of God's will and also strengthen the person to bear the trials that come in the fulfilling of God's purpose.

Christ was not "called" to God's service in the human sense but, even though He is God, He became the obedient servant of God in order to accomplish the Father's will and to save mankind from eternal death. By his example of obedience to the Father's will, He becomes for us a model of how we should respond to God's call. He was fully aware that, through His sacrifice, God's mercy would flow on mankind. He also knew that His sacrifice would be an example to His apostles and all Christians to enable them to continue His saving mission.

When the Angel Gabriel assured the Blessed Mary that the Lord would be with her, he was reminding her of the trials that would come with God's call. Of course, the Blessed Virgin would be aware of the frustrating missions of the prophets in the Old Testament. Again and again, Moses addressed God, expressing his frustrations that the Israelites were becoming ungrateful and forgetful of His mercies to them and were complaining of their material needs for food and water and turning to the worship of idols. Jonah even thought of what he considered to be a wiser idea for God, his Creator. When the Lord sent him to the people of Nineveh to preach repentance to them, he had other ideas. If these gentiles were stubborn, he could not understand why the all-powerful God would waste His time on them. God had the power and the means to destroy them. Jonah forgot about God's mission and disappeared. Of course, God showed that His purpose can never be frustrated.

Jonah was swallowed by the whale for three days and three nights. What is more, God, in His mercy, turned Jonah's disobedience into the greatest sign of our salvation. Christ Himself used Jonah's case as God's miracle to signify His death and resurrection which would rescue the whole of mankind from death. In the scripture, therefore, God uses human struggles to strengthen other souls to do His will and also as examples for humanity to achieve perfection. The Apostle Peter's initial rejection of a crucified Messiah, his abandonment of Christ during His Passion, would not only strengthen him when he led the Church, but would also strengthen all Christians during persecution and times of spiritual misery.

We see Saint Faustina's account of her first frustration at the time she entered the convent. Saint Faustina was experiencing spiritual sweetness as she acquired a deeper knowledge of goodness and beauty and was enjoying prayer when she suddenly saw that her fellow nuns had little time for prayer and that they were lax and undisciplined. Christ came to educate her on the Way of the Cross and sacrifice for sinners: there was no way to God other than the Way of the Cross.

The Voice of God and Transformation of the Soul

When God calls a soul to His service, the graces that He pours into the soul enable insights into supernatural things and into God's secrets. Souls called must therefore be attentive to God's voice, precisely because God is constantly revealing His thoughts which are beyond human knowledge. Christ becomes our perfect model, because during His life on Earth, He always found time to move apart from the crowd and engage in internal recollection to listen to His Father's voice. Christ also went about doing good, and by His merciful living, in effect, brings God's power to Himself.

All Christians are Called

Through baptism, all Christians are called by God in Christ who saved them. By His life, good works and sacrifice, Christ confirmed to mankind that the only way to God is through the fulfilment of God's commandments, which He summarised as love of God and love of neighbour. Christ therefore calls all Christians to love God and neighbour and in the gospel reminds us that we have a very short time in this world to heed His Father's call to salvation.

Christ reveals to mankind, especially Christians, that by His obedience to the Father, the fruit of His sacrifice becomes the Advocate, the Holy Spirit to whom our Spirit is joined. We are joined to the Spirit in Christ, so then we are joined to God and should be able to respond to His will, like Christ, and thus answer His call. Joined to the Spirit in Christ, the Spirit directs us to answer God's call. If all Christians can only be joined to the Spirit in Christ, then there is only one Body and we should consider God's call as enabling us through the gift of the Spirit to fulfil specific roles in Christ's body. As members of the Body of Christ, then, we must see ourselves as serving God in a community of believers (Christians).

Also, by answering the Father's call, we become witnesses to the truth and by charity become the living images of Christ. Saint Faustina's experience can be described as a call addressed to all Christians. We are invited to become participants in Christ's redemptive work through new devotions and return to the gospel message. In this way, collectively and individually, we become instruments of God's grace and salvation. The Diary brings new insights of salvation through Saint Faustina's charity. Saint Faustina's call may be extraordinary but we are called in different ways and circumstances to God's purpose.

CHAPTER 2

Divine Mercy and the Mystery of Holy Trinity: restoring sinful humanity to holiness and glory

Saint Faustina was reflecting on the mystery of the Holy Trinity, particularly on the essence of God. While engaged in these thoughts, the saint describes how she was suddenly confronted with a mystical experience: "In an instant my spirit was caught up into what seemed to be the next world. I saw an inaccessible light, and in this light what appeared like three sources of light which I could not understand. And out of that light came words in the form of lightning which encircled Heaven and earth. Not understanding anything, I was very sad. Suddenly, from this sea of inaccessible light came our dearly beloved Saviour, unutterably beautiful with His shining Wounds. And from this light came a voice which said: 'Who God is in His Essence, no one will fathom, neither the mind of angels nor man.' Jesus said to me: 'Get to know God by contemplating His attributes.' A moment later, He traced the sign of the cross with His hand and vanished." (Diary 30)

Divine Mercy, the most excellent work of the most Holy Trinity

The gift of human redemption flows on mankind from the very depths of the Holy Trinity. In this act of Trinitarian mercy, God the Father sends Christ, His Son, to take human nature and restore sinful humanity into communion with Himself. God the Father uses His Holy Spirit of love (which unites and seals Him to His Son) to distribute gifts to the redeemed in order to sanctify and restore them to Himself.

Why does Christ instruct Saint Faustina not to contemplate Divine Essence?

When the saint was seeking knowledge about Divine Essence, she was seeking to know truths that are not only incomprehensible to man but also those truths that are not immediately necessary for human salvation. She was also seeking answers to matters relating to the sources of the Trinity's power and holy will. Such knowledge is only known by Christ, who has the same substance as God the Father. The human soul, by the death and resurrection of Jesus Christ, is enabled to become the adopted child of God and to participate in His glory. Saint Catherine of Siena summarises the limitations of human knowledge of God as follows: "Eternal Trinity, You are like a deep sea, in which the more I seek, the more I find; and the more I find, the more I seek You." In the divine plan of salvation, humans become partners and sharers in Christ's divine glory by the working of the Holy Spirit. The secrets of God's inner being give life to creation but He reveals such attributes as are necessary for human redemption. The old mystic, St Hildegard, says that certain knowledge is beyond humanity: "There is nothing in humans that can understand the breadth of the Trinity's glory nor the lengths of His power."

A deliberate search to discover God's essence would amount to pride and spiritual rebellion, such as that mounted by the Devil, who sought equality with God. All God's people in whose hearts grace is active are led by the Holy Spirit who offers all the knowledge and understanding necessary for salvation.

Revealed attributes of Trinity necessary for our salvation

Trinity is the source of our life and it is only the Trinitarian presence that can sustain existence and lead us to eternal good. It is therefore spiritually fitting that we know and imitate its attributes.

The most fundamental attribute of the Trinity that is revealed to mankind is that even as three persons truly distinct from one another, it is truly one and it is in an infinite communion of love.

It is from the mystery of this love that humanity was created to enjoy its gratuitous love. The Three Divine Persons work in unity not only to sustain human life but also to restore us to perfection. The entire work of creation, redemption and sanctification comes from the Trinity and all these unified actions have as their purpose the drawing of humanity into communion with God.

The mystery of Divine Unity and love is at work in humans. God the Father, our Creator, is the source of love for all mankind. He reveals this love through his Son, our Lord Jesus Christ, who obeyed the Father and took human nature to redeem mankind. By the Son's sacrifice, the Father, through the Holy Spirit, bestows the graces that guide us to become, in Christ, the children of God. Christ gives us an example of how to make sacrifices for God's glory and to live for and love our fellow human beings. He becomes the way to the inner transformation of the human person in his relationship with God and his fellow man. The action of the Trinity also reveals to us the necessity of forming a human community that moves towards God, our true and final destiny.

Also, in the scripture, God is revealed as holy. Holiness implies not only love but kindness, glory, splendour and righteousness. That quality of God encompasses all that is good, all that sanctifies and all that transforms other spirits and elevates them to grace and glory. The holy attribute of God gives and transforms life but it also creates a deep chasm that can annihilate all souls that are not spiritually aided by God's mercy. Confronted with God's holiness, the sinful man sees the filth of his own soul. According to Isaiah, even angels cover their faces and feet, and feel compelled by this holiness to proclaim aloud the splendour of his glory. Christ, in the light of His divinity, saw, in his human nature, the immense weight of human sins and accepted His cross.

Consequences of God's holiness

God's holiness is eternally opposed to sin, as sin is a rebellion against God's holiness. Sin destroys the soul's movement towards God, infects society and leads to collective wickedness. Sin led to our first parents being thrown out of paradise and sin destroys the holy nature created by God.

God's holiness is infinite and it is only the infinitely holy nature of Christ, in his humanity, that could have redeemed the sinful man.

Divine Mercy and Divine attributes

By the merits of Christ's sacrifice, God offers all repentant sinners the gift of infinite mercy. We must therefore see the messages and devotions of Saint Faustina as a merciful offer and consolation to all souls in their various circumstances of life, especially if they are in despair because they fear God's justice.

Benefits of contemplation

By imitating Christ's life, humans are enabled to begin their heavenly existence even in this life, to be fully revealed in the next. In Christ, God restores souls to Himself.

To enjoy the spiritual fruits of contemplation, we must endeavour to know the revealed nature and attributes of the Trinity, working in unity for our salvation. St John of the Cross explains that knowledge of the Trinity opens our souls to God's indwelling within us and makes us ready to be guided into the supernatural life. St Gregory of Nyssa also believes that knowing God's attributes comes naturally to souls. According to the saint, if we are purified of disordered affections, we see within us the image of the divine nature. He concludes: "It is purity, sanctity, simplicity and other such luminous reflections of the divine nature, in which God is contemplated."

Other saints offer routes to the discovery of divine attributes. St Thomas Aquinas says that since these revealed truths of God are supernatural and exceed human reason, we should accept them by faith and see them as signs of God and the blessed and that they manifest the divine role in human acts. St Catherine of Siena adds that the reasoning process that leads to the discovery of the divine nature should not be regarded as mere abstract reasoning, since abstract reasoning cannot lead us to eternal truths, but that we require purity of heart to get to know God's attributes. Purity of heart, according to the saint, can only be obtained by the practice of Christian virtues which then facilitates our spiritual movement towards God. "It is not the tongue, it is the unction of grace which teaches these things; they are hidden from the great and the wise of this world, but God reveals them to babes."

To know and grow in the knowledge of divine attributes that produce the graces necessary for spiritual perfection and salvation, we need a proper spiritual disposition acquired through prayer, good works and trust.

The Trinity and the Soul

Saint Faustina recounts an experience in which the Blessed Trinity helped her to overcome the darkness she saw in her soul. She writes as follows: "It seemed as though hell had conspired against me. A terrible hatred began to break out in my soul, hatred for all that is holy and divine. It seemed to me that these spiritual torments would be my lot for the rest of my life. I turned to the Blessed Sacrament and said to Jesus, 'Jesus, my Spouse, do You not see that my soul is dying because of its longing for You? How can You hide Yourself from a heart that loves You so sincerely. Forgive me, Jesus; may Your holy will be done in me. I will suffer silently like a dove, without complaining. I will not allow my heart even one single cry of sorrowful complaint." (Diary 25)

Saint Faustina writes about this experience to enlighten us about how she trusted in the Trinity to help her to overcome a period of darkness in her soul. In the end she was grateful to God that her soul was gradually transformed with the help of the Trinitarian light. Saint Faustina's experience reminds us of the scripture account of Christ's agony in the garden. He entered into a deep contemplation before His Heavenly Father as, in His agony, He confronted the darkness of this world. In the end, He entrusted His contest with evil to the will of His Heavenly Father and was able to go ahead and conquer the challenge of the cross.

Saint Peter in his first letter describes souls as chosen by the "provident purpose of God the Father, to be made Holy by the Spirit, obedient to Jesus Christ and sprinkled with his blood." Saint Peter explains that it is the will of God the Father which calls each and every one of us to holiness and that in responding to this call we are guided by the Holy Spirit with the power of discernment of God's purpose. He refers to the example of Our Lord Jesus Christ, the Wisdom and Source of our life, who came into the world so that by His life and passion He would show us the way to fulfil the Father's purpose. He said Christ showed us the way to submit to divine will by His life, death and resurrection. He cautions us that for a time, we will be plagued by all kinds of trials so that when Jesus Christ is revealed, our faith will have been tested and proven like gold. We can see the effect of Christ's appearance in the transformation that Saint Faustina experienced when she encountered Christ. Saint Augustine explains the confrontation with the dark forces of this world as a self-emptying process which is necessary for humans to encounter, to enable God to bestow the graces necessary for perfection in us. He puts it this way: "Consider that God wants to fill you up with honey, but if you are already full of vinegar, where will you put the honey? What was in the vessel must be emptied out; the vessel itself must be washed out and made clean and scoured, hard though it may be, so that it be made fit for something else, whatever it may be."

We learn from Saint Faustina's experience that we need constantly to renew ourselves in God by fighting against ourselves through renunciation of our weaknesses and the ways of the world in order to achieve unity with God.

CHAPTER 3

The Blessed Virgin Mary:
the power and splendour of Divine Mercy

From the history of salvation and the traditions of the Church, it has been established that God has willed to accomplish his designs of salvation and manifest his mercy with the active participation of the Blessed Virgin Mary. God's designs were not only revealed in the Old Testament but also in the revelation of His only begotten Son, Our Lord Jesus Christ. Mary's image was prepared in the Old Testament and God used her in the manifestation of His earthly power through His Son.

John Paul II in the encyclical "Dives in Misericordia" describes Mary as "Mary the Mother of Mercy." It was explained in that encyclical that Mary, having obtained rich mercy, uses her first-hand experience to spread the message of mercy in this life and continues to co-operate with God in our redemption.

From the scripture story of the fall of man, it has been implied by the Fathers of the Church that God had Mary in mind when He saw that He would bring enmity between the Woman's seed and Satan.

Mary would therefore be an instrument through which the Devil would be conquered and man rescued from sin. If Mary is the Queen of Mercy, it is because she was assigned by God at the time He declared mercy on mankind to be a principal participant in the mysterious rescue of mankind. It is no wonder that during the famous Magnificat, Mary saw herself as the greatest beneficiary of God's mercy for mankind. She inwardly saw herself elevated to the Motherhood of God and the most blessed among all creation. Indeed the Gospel confirms her extraordinary position as the greatest sharer of the life of the Holy Trinity. She would co-operate with the Holy

Spirit to give birth to the Son of the Most High. The birth of Christ was confirmed by the miracle of the bright star and the revelation to gentiles.

Saint Faustina recorded in her diary that she was asked by Christ always to seek the help of the Blessed Virgin Mary. As the greatest human beneficiary of the Divine Mercy, Mary becomes a true model for any Christian who seeks the way of perfection.

Saint Faustina and the Blessed Virgin Mary

Saint Faustina recorded in her diary that the Blessed Virgin Mary addressed her as follows: "I am not only the Queen of Heaven, but also the Mother of Mercy and your Mother" (Diary 330).

From the moment that the saint had the vision of her call to sanctity, she became devoted to the Mother of God and always sought her help. Before she took her perpetual vows, she knew of the necessity of Our Lady's help and prayed as follows: "You have to love me. Oh Mary, My Dearest Mother, guide my spiritual life in such a way that it will please your Son" (Diary 240). The saint later added: "I entrusted my perpetual vows to her. I felt that I was her child and that she was my Mother. She did not refuse any of my requests." (Diary 260) It was her practice to prepare and participate in the feasts of Our Lady. Before the feast of Assumption, she recorded as follows: "Today, I started a novena to Our Lady of the Assumption for three intentions: first, that I may see the Reverend Dr Sopocko; second, that God would hasten this work; and third, for the intention of my country" (Diary 1206).

Her devotion to Our Lady brought her enormous graces, as she once noted: "Today [7th December 1937] is the Eve of the Feast of the Immaculate Conception of the Virgin Mary. During the midday meal, in an instant, God gave me to know the greatness of my destiny; that is, His closeness, which for all eternity will not be taken away from me, and He did this in such a vivid and clear fashion that I remained wrapped up in His living presence for a long time, humbling myself before His greatness" (Diary 1410).

The Saint's devotion to the Mother of God enabled her to develop special prayers to her. An example is as follows: "O sweet Mother of God, I model my life on you; You are for me the bright dawn; In you I lose myself, enraptured." (Diary 1232) "O Mary, my sweet Mother, to you I turn over my soul, my body and my poor heart. Be the safeguard of my life, especially at death's hour, in the final fight" (Diary 161).

Mary as the Mother of Mercy in Saint Faustina's Diary

Just as the salvation of mankind was revealed to Mary by the Angel Gabriel during the Annunciation, so the seriousness of the Divine Mercy mission was revealed to the Mother of God in heaven. Our Lady revealed that the purpose of the Divine Mercy apostolate was to prepare the world for the second coming of Christ. He disclosed the following revelations to Saint Faustina: "As for you, you have to speak to the world about His great mercy and prepare the world for the Second Coming of Him who will come, not as a merciful Saviour, but as a just Judge…Speak to souls about this great mercy while it is still the time for (granting) mercy" (Diary 635). Indeed the seriousness of the message can be seen from the fact that no human being has ever received the daily attention of Our Lady as Saint Faustina did.

Our Lady as teacher and guide to the apostle of Divine Mercy

In Our Lady's role as the teacher and guide of mercy, she instructs Saint Faustina about the sacrifices needed to be able to accomplish her mission. On the day of the Feast of the Assumption, the Mother of God appeared to Saint Faustina and advised as follows: "My daughter, what I demand from you is prayer, prayer, and once again prayer, for the world and especially for your country. For nine days receive Holy Communion in atonement and unite yourself closely to the Holy Sacrifice of the Mass. During these nine days you will stand before God as an offering; always and everywhere, at all times and places, day or night, whenever you wake up, pray in the spirit. In spirit, one can always remain in prayer." (Diary 325) For Our Lady, the will of God is paramount as she later told the saint during another vision: "Put the will of God before all sacrifices and holocausts." (Diary 1244) Our Lady further instructs Saint Faustina on the highest virtues needed to accomplish God's will. He recommends the following to Saint Faustina: "I desire, my dearly beloved daughter, that you practise the three virtues that are dearest to me – and most pleasing to God. The first is humility, humility, and once again humility; the second virtue, purity; the third virtue, love of God. As my daughter, you must especially radiate with these virtues." (Diary 1415) The saint disclosed that after Our Lady had spoken to her, she felt that these virtues had been engraved in her heart.

Another advice that Our Lady gave to Saint Faustina was that she should always have the cross in her mind. She describes the encounter as follows: "All at once, I saw the image in some small chapel and at that moment I saw that the chapel became an enormous and beautiful temple. And in this temple I saw the Mother of God with the Infant in her arms. And a moment later, the Infant Jesus disappeared from the arms of His Mother, and I saw the living image of Jesus Crucified. The Mother of God told me to do what she had done, that even when joyful, I should always keep my eyes fixed on the cross, and she told me that the graces God was granting me were not for me alone, but for other souls as well." (Diary 561)

Throughout the diary, Saint Faustina discloses that she needed the constant protection, guidance and instruction of Our Lady because she realized her human weakness and spiritual inexperience and that Our Lady's help made her feel at peace and close to her Immaculate Heart. She describes the effect of Mary's help as follows: "My spirit brightens up in your gentleness and your humility, O Mary." (Diary 620) Mary indeed was the apostle's instructress in the mysteries of the Divine Mercy.

Mary and the Old Testament

In his introduction to the "Lumen Gentium", Cardinal Paul Poupard describes Mary's motherhood of the People of God as follows: "Already begun but not yet complete, it is a mystical communion, a People of God seeking to live in holiness and communion under the loving gaze of the Mother of God who looks on her with the same tenderness with which she looked on her crucified Son, seeing in it, the reflection of her offspring's life of sacrifice, devotion and celebration." God reveals Mary's role in His plan of Salvation in the Old Testament through prophets, holy people, events and signs. The inspired word of the Bible needed to gradually unfold Mary's role for a number of reasons. God is all knowing and all powerful but in His designs and dealings with humanity, He unfolds all His plans and does not take man by surprise. He would not reveal the promise of the Messiah without at the same time revealing how this plan would be accomplished.

The revelation of Mary in the Old Testament was a necessary means for God to manifest his power and mercy. To redeem mankind, God would need to defeat Satan by reversing his rebellion and conquering him to effect the restoration of mankind to his original glory. God needed to hint at the creation of a holy Eve who would be the incorruptible vessel of the Messiah's entry into the world. In contrast with Eve, the created holy woman would defeat Satan and be the new mother of redeemed humanity.

Women in the Old Testament would be less holy than Mary as individuals but they would gradually unfold the perfect Mary, the woman envisaged by God, who would co-operate with God to save mankind. The idea of the holy woman conceived by God would therefore be women responding to God's word of holy living. By their character, the women-types of the Old Testament would promote God's glory and point to His merciful love for humanity; they would show humility and display heroic virtue, which is necessary for salvation; they would show their capacity for leadership in the exercise of holy charity. These women would also lead people to collective praise and worship of God. Finally, if the people of Israel perceived the female sex as weak, God unfolded through these women that the weak, the humble and the oppressed would be His instruments of triumph and glory.

We can now examine a few cases of Mary's links to the Old

Testament. Most significantly when Adam and Eve were being expelled from paradise, God promised to crush the head of the serpent using a woman. The Fathers of the Church take this as a reference to Mary. Isaiah refers to the sign of a virgin birth and the accession to the throne of David by a child who receives human and divine names. God promised the everlasting dynasty of a virgin's child who would be called Emmanuel, meaning God with us. Also, the prophet Micah refers to a royal motherhood and a daughter of Zion giving birth in pain and leading to the redemption from enemies. The story of Judith is about a victory won by the chosen people of God over their enemies, thanks to the intervention of a holy woman. The Jewish nation was facing the mighty army of Holofernes, who aimed at bringing the whole world under Nebuchadnezzar and destroying all other religions except that of the deified Nebuchadnezzar. The Jews had been besieged and were on the point of surrender. Judith, a beautiful young widow, who was also devout, overcame the cowardice of her own people. She rebuked the leading men of the city for their lack of faith in God. She took to prayer, went to meet Holofernes and using all her charms and wit, made him drunk and cut off his head. The Assyrian enemy was defeated; the people of God sang the praises of Judith and returned to Jerusalem for thanksgiving. In this story, Judith, who was a holy woman of God, becomes God's instrument to overcome the incarnation of the powers of evil. Judith's triumph can be seen as the reward of prayer, purity and total trust in God. Thus the weak woman who trusts in God triumphs over evil. The high priests of Israel celebrated the victory with the following words:

> You are the glory of Jerusalem!
> You are the great pride of Israel!
> You are the highest honour of our race!

Likewise in the book of Esther, we are told of how the holy woman Esther delivered God's people of Israel from their deadly enemy. The Jews who had settled in Persia were being threatened with extermination by Haman, a hostile and all powerful king. She was able to convince the monstrous king, Ahuerus, who instead ordered that Haman should be hanged and the position given to Esther's cousin; thus the Jews were spared. Again, as in the case of Judith, Esther trusted in God to work out the salvation of her people. Also, as in the case of Judith, Esther's humble prayers were significant:

> Oh God, whose strength prevails over all,
> Listen to the voice of the desperate,
> Save us from the hand of the wicked,
> And free me from my fear!

In conclusion, Judith, Esther and some other holy women foreshadowed the Virgin Mary, the holiest of women who would be the Mother of God.

The Blessed Virgin Mary and the New Testament

Christ revealed in the New Testament that He came to fulfil the prophecies of the Old Testament. The gospel writers were careful to ascribe the old prophecies that pointed to the life and death of Christ. In a similar way, we can identify close associations with Mary's participation in the fulfilment of Christ's salvific mission. Mary's participation in Christ's mission of salvation is so central that St Bernard would say as follows: "Mary is not newly discovered nor by chance, but chosen from all ages, foreknown by the Most High and prepared for Himself, guarded by angels, prefigured by the Fathers and promised by the prophets." The circumstances of Mary's birth and call, as well as her heroic response to God's mercy, contribute to fulfil God's redemptive plans in Christ.

At the Annunciation, Mary was entrusted with a mission that was conveyed by God's messenger, the Angel Gabriel; it was similar to the mission that confronted the Old Testament prophets Moses, Jeremiah, Amos and John the Baptist. The Angel Gabriel disclosed that Mary was a special beneficiary of God's favour. Her mission was to co-operate with the Holy Spirit to give birth to the Son of God, the promised Messiah who would free people from their sins.

The angel's greeting addressing Mary as "Full of Grace" (Luke 1:28) is unique in the Bible and was reserved exclusively for the Virgin Mary. It confirms that in the divine plan, eternally linked to Christ, a special place has been reserved for the Mother of God. In this regard we are reminded of God's warning at the fall of man that there would be enmity between the woman's seed and Satan's seed (Gen. 3:15). The Annunciation was therefore a transcendent event, raising Mary to participate with the Trinity in the most significant event of God's mercy. Mary freely submitted to God's will and was willing to co-operate with the Holy Spirit to give birth to the Son of God. In this regard, it can be said that Mary was a great sign, not an ordinary mother. This is why the Catechism of the Catholic Church asserts as follows: "In fact, the One whom she conceived as man by the Holy Spirit, who truly became her Son according to the flesh, was none other than the Father's eternal Son, the Second person of the Holy Trinity. Hence the Church confesses that Mary is truly Mother of God." The angel's message has its roots in the Old Testament prophecies. The child would be Jesus; He would be the Son of the Most High; the Son of David, the King of Israel; The Promised Messiah. The Virgin Mary responds to the honour with humility and faith. She understands that her blessedness is an act of God's merciful love and that the task entrusted to her was the salvation of the world and beyond all human power. The words used by the angel all have significant meanings in the Old Testament. "Full of Grace" is a spiritual blessing which she would receive from the Trinity through Jesus Christ to be poured on humanity. It is an everlasting favour for Mary and for all the chosen people of God. Also, the angel's greeting "Hail Mary" in the Bible, is an expression of messianic joy, as announced by the prophets to the "Daughter of Zion", personification of the remnant of Israel: "Shout for joy, Oh Daughter of Zion! Sing joyfully Oh Israel. The Lord your God is with you, a mighty Saviour." (Zeph. 3:14)

The name of Mary refers to Miriam in the Old Testament and was the name of the sister of Moses and Aaron, who led the singing and thanksgiving at the crossing of the Red Sea (Ex. 15). Also, in the Old Testament, God says to Moses, who was fearful of the task entrusted to him: "I will be with you" (Ex 3:12). So when the angel spoke the words "The Lord is with you", he was assuring her that even though the task entrusted to her was beyond all human power, yet nothing was impossible to God.

Another Old Testament association with Our Lady's call occurred during her visit to Elizabeth. In what is famously described as the Magnificat, Mary used a psalm of thanksgiving from the Old Testament. By her prayer of thanksgiving, she put herself totally at the service of the people of God. In her and by her, salvation is announced. In her poverty, the beatitude is announced: a humble faith which would be deepened through trials and temptations. The Magnificat also recalls the story of Hannah, a woman of God in the Old Testament. She was the mother of Samuel, who offered her son to God and he later became a prophet. In a song she sung as she dedicated her child to the Lord's service, she uttered these words: "The Lord makes poor and makes rich; He brings low and lifts up. He raises the poor from the dust and lifts the beggar from the ash heap...The Lord will judge the ends of the earth." (1 Samuel 2:7-8). So we can see that Mary was inspired by the Holy Spirit to draw her words from Hannah and Psalm 75 (see Luke 1:52-53). From the visit to Elizabeth, we can see that from the moment of her conception, Mary is already a participant in the Trinitarian plan of redemption, being acknowledged by Elizabeth who already discerns that Mary is the Mother of God.

At the birth of Christ, we witnessed Mary's humble circumstances and the fact that the humiliating birth in the stable does not diminish her love of God. Even though from the lineage of the rich and powerful Saint David, she has no rich inheritance and this would seem to indicate that the Son of God had come into the world to be identified with the poor and the oppressed. However, in spite of Christ's humble birth, the divinity of Christ is revealed by angels chanting his glory. Mary becomes a witness of her Son's universal kingship; she responds with heroic generosity to God's graces and becomes a perfect image of her Creator.

At the presentation in the temple, Mary is made fully aware of her own role in the fulfilment of the Old Testament prophecies. She hears the prophecies of the servant of God applied to her Son, a light to the nations and a sign of contradiction. Even though she is told of the mysteries of redemption by Simeon (inspired by the Holy Spirit), she quietly but heroically keeps all these things in her heart (Luke 2:19).

Mary gradually accepts that her Son has to be allowed and helped to fulfil God's mission of redemption. We see at the presentation in the temple that Simeon announces her son's true mission as the servant of God. So while she exercises responsibility over her divine Son, she heroically learns to accept suffering if she is to help her Son to obey God. According to Luke, at the age of twelve years, Jesus tells his earthly parents that he belongs first of all to his heavenly Father (Luke 2:49). This abandonment of her Son to God's mission and to fulfil the scripture will be completed on the cross. When Jesus addresses Mary as the "woman", He establishes Himself as the Lord of the Kingdom. And by designating to His Mother the disciple who was present, "behold your Son", Jesus calls her to a new maternity, which will be her new role for the people of God. This role continues when Our Lady is at prayer with the twelve awaiting the Spirit. That event marks the birth of the Church and her own universal motherhood. Mary, by closely uniting her sacrifices with those of her Son, becomes a victim whose sacrifices are accepted by God. She becomes the Mother of Sorrows, giving birth in this life to children of suffering souls. So we can say that the Old Testament prophecies of human redemption are fulfilled in Christ closely uniting himself with His mother.

Our Lady's accomplishment of God's merciful designs of salvation in her children

During her life on Earth, Mary acquired the most perfect merits conceivable by submitting to God's will to redeem humanity through her participation in Christ's redemptive actions, imitating her Son's virtues by keeping all that she saw in her heart and through her life giving glory to God the Father who had done great things for her. Mary did receive God's mercy and responded perfectly to His mercy. Her earthly actions therefore made her a great powerhouse of God that generated light for souls even in heaven. Mary's role in salvation can therefore be described as a pre-ordained sign of God's power which lights up human hearts. By imitating the life of Mary, all faithful souls can, like her, become participants in God's plan of salvation. Faithful souls who follow the Blessed Virgin Mary become like Christ and have been described by Saint Chrysologus as "Heaven on earth, earth in heaven, man in God, God in man."

So even in heaven, Mary continues to do great things for the salvation of mankind. It has been established that the faithful who ask for her help during trials, sufferings or temptations receive great help. Also, persons who have been very devoted to her are able to perform heroic works and become great saints. A few examples of her intervention from Heaven have been selected to illustrate this point.

St Philomena

St Philomena had the ambition even as a young girl to die for Christ. However, around the year 302, Diocletian, the new emperor of Rome, started to persecute her father Calistos, who was a governor. Diocletian threatened to kill Philomena's parents but said he would only spare them if they would allow him to marry Philomena. Philomena bluntly told the emperor that she was consecrated to Christ forever. She said that on her first Communion, she had vowed her virginity to Christ and she would follow the example of the Blessed Virgin Mary. Philomena was arrested by the emperor and chained in a cell. She was whipped to the point when she was expected to die. She underwent several forms of torture, including being tied in chains and her body riddled with arrows.

Our Lady, however, answered her prayer for help. While she prayed in her cell, she saw Our Lady emerging from a light brighter than the sun. She assured her that even though she would suffer greatly for three days, Jesus would help her and that she had commanded the

Angel Gabriel to watch over her. She also assured her that Jesus had prepared an everlasting glory for her and that angels were waiting to take her to heaven. Philomena saw Mary with the Divine Child who placed Him into Philomena's arms to console her.

When finally Philomena's head was placed on a block and she was beheaded with an axe, all those present during her ordeal saw a halo of light around her head and that light rose gradually into Heaven and disappeared on Friday, 10th August 302 at 3 pm.

St John Damascene

This saint inherited a great fortune from his father, even though he himself was well educated and greatly honoured in his community. He gave up his wealth to the poor and went to live in a monastery near Jerusalem as a monk and priest.

When Emperor Leo III ordered that all sacred images should be destroyed, St Damascene publicly opposed the emperor's order. The emperor accused him of treason and his right hand was cut off and displayed publicly.

St John Damascene prayed to Our Lady for help. He implored Our Lady to heal him, to restore his hand so that he could write her praises and those of her divine son. Following that prayer, Our Lady appeared to St John Damascene and assured him that his hand had been restored.

The emperor who saw the miracle then became convinced that St John Damascene was right on the question of sacred images and he was restored to the emperor's favour. With his right hand restored, the saint was able to write many sermons and hymns and has become a Doctor of the Church.

St Monica

Saint Monica's husband was a pagan who treated her badly. Her son Augustine led an immoral life and rejected her religion. She therefore turned to the Blessed Virgin Mary for help and prayed to her constantly.

Our Lady appeared to Saint Monica dressed in mourning with

a cincture tied around her waist. However, the cincture shone brightly. She asked Saint Monica to dress herself as she (Mary) was dressed. Mary gave the cincture to Monica and told her never to remove it.

Later, Augustine was converted and received baptism from Saint Ambrose. He later became a bishop and wrote many spiritual works.

St Bernard of Clairvaux

As a monk, St Bernard was devoted to his God but he suffered from poor health and experienced pains that interfered with his devotions. In desperation, he requested two fellow monks to go to the Church and pray for his healing.

While the monks who were praying for him, prostrating themselves before the statues of the Virgin Mary, St Benedict and St Lawrence, Our Lady and the two saints appeared to St Bernard in his cell. They all touched St Bernard's body and he was immediately healed.

From the time he was healed, St Bernard became a great devotee of the Virgin Mary. His works on the Blessed Virgin Mary are very deep and have contributed greatly to Marian devotion.

St Dominic

St Dominic was greatly devoted to the Virgin Mary. Like Mary, he loved souls, especially sinners. He was therefore distressed by the Albigensian heresy. The Albigensians believed that because all matter was evil, Christ could never have become fully human because to do so would be to fall into corruption. St Dominic therefore prayed in the chapel of Notre-Dame de la Prouille to the Virgin Mary to save the Church from the heresy. Our Lady appeared to St Dominic and gave him the rosary and asked him to promote devotion to the rosary.

Led by Simone de Montfort, the Catholic Church waged war against the heretics. Even though the Albigensians greatly outnumbered the soldiers of Simone de Montfort, they were defeated and after the war, the heresy disappeared. The Church soldiers used the rosary throughout the campaign.

St Dominic laboured to promote the rosary; his Order, the Dominicans, spread throughout the world and the power of the rosary has featured in the history of the Church.

St Rose of Lima

St Rose at first made up her mind to join the Augustinian convent but first she went to the rosary altar of a Dominican church to pray to Our Lady; she suddenly realised that she could not move from the spot where she was praying. She then began to think that the Virgin Mary was asking her to remain with the Dominicans. The moment she decided to remain in that convent, a strange force released her from the spot. She was admitted as a novice in the third order of St Dominic.

At the start of her new vocation, she entrusted herself to Mary to be a perfect Dominican. Our Lady in fact visited her and guided her. She was eventually mystically betrothed to Christ. Also in a mystical way, she knew the time of her death. Before her death, she visited her parents and asked for their blessings; she asked everybody for a greater love of God, also asking pardon for all her faults. Finally, she requested to be allowed to sleep on the bare floor so that she might die like Christ. She then died, saying "Jesus, Jesus, be with me."

The Great signs confirming the Spiritual Motherhood of the Blessed Virgin Mary: Lourdes and Fatima

In His plan to restore humanity to goodness and salvation, God willed to use the Blessed Virgin Mary to remind humanity of His mercy in the two dramatic events that took place in Lourdes and Fatima. In both events, which occurred in France and Portugal respectively, God used little children to transform villages that were previously unrecognised and made them centres where people would flock to listen to the Word of God, be reminded of their erring ways and move in the path of repentance. Signs and miracles would accompany the merciful designs of God that were proclaimed by the Blessed Virgin Mary in the two places of pilgrimage.

The Blessed Virgin Mary appeared eighteen times to a simple

little girl called Bernadette between February and July 1858 at a place in France called Massabielle, meaning "Old Rock". In a rocky cave, Bernadette saw a lady dressed in white with a blue sash and a yellow rose on each foot, the colour of her rosary.

The message of Bernadette was at first not taken seriously; her poor parents were illiterate who could not afford to send her to school. Bernadette's father, François Soubirous, his wife, Louise, and their four children lived in an abandoned prison building. Bernadette's messages from Our Lady were therefore ridiculed. The police and the public authorities arrested her because she was viewed as creating unnecessary commotion in the locality.

Lourdes, however, manifested the simplicity and poverty of the bible environment. Bernadette was a poor, sickly child who would manifest God's love for the powerless and the weak. The rock and cave of Massabielle, located at the foot of Pyrenean Mountains, reflected the rock of the psalms which in the Bible reflects the strength of God who is faithful to the people of Israel. The mountain setting also reflects the bible description of the mountain as God's dwelling place. The cave located within the mountain is where in the bible the Divine Presence is revealed. The prophets Moses and Elijah are described as being in God's presence in the cave. We also find that the incarnation setting is the cave at Bethlehem where gentiles are attracted by the star to go and worship God in the manger. The water which would appear at Lourdes to heal pilgrims reflects our baptism and life in the Spirit. Water cleanses us of our sins to begin a new life in the kingdom of God.

There is also the mysterious appearance of water at Lourdes, which has been a main attraction. On 25th February 1858, St Bernadette was appearing before Our Lady and was engaged in conversation with her. Suddenly, at the back of the grotto, she was seen to be kissing the ground several times. With her right hand, she scooped mud from the ground and smeared her face with the wet red mud and then she swallowed the muddy liquid. She also picked some weeds growing at the back of the grotto and chewed them. The public saw clear water coming out of the little hole from which

Bernadette had scooped the mud. Since then, this water has become the Miraculous Lourdes Water.

The strange actions of Bernadette that led to the appearance of water were meant by Our Lady to manifest the need for penance and a form of expiation for sinners.

Our Lady confirms the doctrine of the Immaculate Conception

In March 1858 at the feast of the Annunciation, during her meeting with the Blessed Virgin Mary, St Bernadette asked Our Lady who she was and she replied: "I am the Immaculate Conception". Not knowing what it meant, Bernadette kept repeating the words and rushed to communicate the words to the parish priest, adding that Our Lady wanted a chapel to be built. The circumstances of the revelation shocked the Church and led to great belief in the message of Lourdes. The doctrine confirms that Our Lady was full of grace because she was without sin when she accepted God's call for her and humanity. She was therefore fit to become the Spiritual Mother of the new humanity and model for all who accept God's call and renounce Satan. The Motherhood of Mary in salvation history was therefore confirmed at Lourdes. Humanity is called at Lourdes to offer sacrifices that will lead to the triumph over evil. It is appropriate that since her death, St Bernadette has been honoured with an incorruptible body. Forty-six years after she died, her body was exhumed on 18th April 1925. When the body was examined, it had not undergone decomposition and was incorrupt. In her black clothes, her hands were still holding rosary beads. She has since been placed in a glass case and the incorrupt body can be seen today in a convent in Nevers.

The Fatima Apparitions

The case of Fatima manifests the same biblical setting as Lourdes. Here there were three little children of which the eldest, Lucia, was only ten. Like Lucia the other two, Francisco and Jacinta, were shepherds. They had been brought up in the traditions of the village, looking after sheep and taking breaks to say the Angelus and the Rosary.

The miraculous events took place in 1917, the year of the communist revolution in Russia and the beginning of state persecution of Christians. The Communists had as their goal the ideology of materialism and state-sponsored atheism.

Like Lourdes, Our Lady came to Fatima in Portugal to remind humanity that God is our true origin and destination as contained in the scripture. Mankind is also reminded that sin is rebellion that leads to hell and that Man should take the gospel message seriously. Humanity is reminded that God's mercy is still at work but that human ingratitude was offending God. Our Lady would ask the faithful not just to pray for themselves but to make sacrifices for sinful humanity.

Another important message which God wished to proclaim to the world at Fatima was the place of the Virgin Mary in His plan of redemption. The world should recognize her as the Mother of God and as the Mother whose heart, like her Son's, was pierced with a lance. The world should therefore recognize her and not blaspheme against her. Indeed they are to consecrate themselves to the Immaculate Heart of Mary. She was revealed as a participant in her Son's redemptive work. New devotions would prepare mankind to participate in God's plan of restoring her to her true position as the mother of the new humanity.

The events of Fatima are summarized here from the accounts of Lucia, one of the children: "After having taken our lunch and said our prayers, we began to see, some distance off, above the trees that stretched away towards the east, a light, whiter than snow, in the form of a young man, transparent, and brighter than crystal pierced by the rays of the sun. As he drew nearer, we could distinguish his features more and more clearly. We were surprised, absorbed, and struck dumb with amazement." (Fatima in Lucia's own words.)
The angel uttered the following prayers:

"My God, I believe, I adore, I hope and I love You. I ask pardon of You for those who do not believe, do not adore, do not hope and do not love You!"

Lucia adds that they were all "led by a supernatural impulse" to repeat the prayer. She adds further that the supernatural atmosphere created was so intense that they nearly forgot their existence, "remaining in the same posture in which he had left us, and continually repeating the same prayer".

The second apparition

The angel appeared. He spoke: "Pray! Pray very much. The Hearts of Jesus and Mary have designs of mercy on you. Offer prayers and sacrifices to the Most High." He explained further: "Make of everything you can a sacrifice, and offer it to God as an act of reparation for the sins by which He is offended, and in supplication for the conversion of sinners. You will thus draw down peace upon your country. I am its guardian angel, the Angel of Portugal. Above all, accept and bear with submission, the suffering which the Lord will send you."

Lucia explains the effects of the prayer: "These words were indelibly impressed on our minds. They were like a light which made us understand who God is, how He loves us and desires to be loved, the value of sacrifice, how pleasing it is to Him and how on account of it, He grants the grace of conversion to sinners."

Third appearance of the Angel

The children had just said the rosary and the prayer the angel had taught them.

"The angel appeared for the third time, holding a chalice in his hands, with a host above it from which some drops of blood were falling into the sacred vessel. Leaving the chalice and the host suspended in the air, the angel prostrated on the ground and repeated this prayer three times:

'Most Holy Trinity, Father, Son and Holy Spirit, I adore You profoundly, and I offer You the most precious Body, Blood, Soul and Divinity of Jesus Christ, present in all the tabernacles of the world, in reparation for the outrages, sacrileges and indifference with which He himself is offended. And, through the infinite merits of His most Sacred Heart, and the Immaculate Heart of Mary, I beg of You the conversion of poor sinners.'"

Rising, the angel took the chalice and the Host in his hands, and then gave the host to Lucia and the contents of the chalice to Francisco and Jacinta, saying the following:

"Take and drink the Body and Blood of Jesus Christ, horribly outraged by ungrateful men. Repair their crimes and console your God!"

The angel then repeated the first prayer, "Most Holy Trinity".

Lucy describes the effects of the third angel encounter: "Impelled by the power of the supernatural that enveloped us, we imitated all that the angel had done, prostrating ourselves on the ground as he did and repeating the prayers that he said. The force of the presence of God was so intense that it absorbed us and almost completely annihilated us. The peace and happiness which we felt were great, but wholly interior, for our souls were completely immersed in God. The physical exhaustion that came over us was also great."

The Apparitions of Our Lady: first apparition on 13th May 1917

Lucia narrated that high on the slopes in the Cova da Tria, there was a flash of lightning; the children saw Our Lady dressed in white (on a small holm oak):

"She was more brilliant than the sun, and radiated a light more clear and intense than a crystal glass filled with sparkling waters when the rays of the burning sun shine through it."

Our Lady confirmed to the children that she was from heaven. For the next six months in succession, she would be meeting them at the same place (on the thirteenth day of every month). The children wanted to know the whereabouts of their two friends who had died; Our Lady replied that one was in heaven while the other was in purgatory.

Our Lady requested the children offer themselves to God. God would send sufferings and trials as an act of reparation for the sins by which He is offended and as supplication for the conversion of sinners.

When the children agreed, Our Lady disclosed to them that they would have much to suffer. Their suffering refers to the initial doubts from their family and the public and their own penances. Our Lady assured them of God's grace which would comfort them. Before her departure, Our Lady seems to have transmitted them God's grace (is she not the mediatrix of all God's graces?) Lucia describes this transmission as follows:

"Our Lady opened the hands for the first time, communicating to us a light so intense that, as it streamed from her hands, its rays penetrated our hearts and the innermost depths of our souls, making us see ourselves in God, who was that light, more clearly than we see ourselves in the best of mirrors. Then, moved by an interior impulse that was also communicated to us, we fell on our knees, repeating in our hearts. "O Most Holy Trinity, I adore You! My God, my God I love in the most Blessed Sacrament."

Finally Lucy describes what happened after the promise:

"As Our Lady spoke these last words, she opened her hands and for the second time, she communicated to us the rays of that same immense light we saw ourselves in, thus, as it were immersed in God. Jacinta and Francisco seemed to be in that part of the light which rose toward heaven, and in that which was poured out on the earth. In front of the palm of Our Lady's right hand was a heart encircled by thorns which pierced it. We understood that this was the Immaculate Heart of Mary, outraged by the sins of humanity and seeking reparation."

At her second apparition Our Lady asked the children:

"Pray the Rosary every day in honour of Our Lady of the Rosary, in order to obtain peace for the world; only she can help you."

In the third apparition, the children were asked to continue to come on the thirteenth of every month until October, when she would perform a miracle for all to see and believe.

She finally requested as follows:

"Sacrifice yourselves for sinners and say many times, especially whenever you make some sacrifice: O Jesus, it is for love of You, for the conversion of sinners, and in reparation for the sins committed against the Immaculate Heart of Mary."

Our Lady allowed the children to have a vision of hell:

Lucy describes as follows: "As Our Lady spoke these last words, she opened her hands once more, as she had done during the previous months. The rays of light seemed to penetrate the earth, and we saw as it were a sea of fire. Plunged in this fire were demons and souls in human form, like transparent embers all blackened or burnished bronze, floating about in the conflagration, now raised into the air by flames that rushed from within themselves together with great clouds of smoke now falling on every side like sparks in huge fires, without weight or equilibrium, amid shrieks and groans of pain and despair, which horrified us and made us tremble with fear (It must have been this sight which caused me to cry out, as people say they heard me). The demons could be distinguished by their terrifying and repellent likeness to frightful and unknown animals, black and transparent like burning coals. Terrified and as if to plead for succour, we looked up at Our Lady, who said to us, so kindly and sadly, 'You have seen hell where the souls of poor sinners go. To save them, God wishes to establish in the world devotion to my Immaculate Heart. If what I say to you is done, many souls will be saved and there will be peace. The war is going to end; but if people do not cease offending God, a worse one will break out during the pontificate of Pius XI.'"

Our Lady requested that Russia should be consecrated to the Immaculate Heart; that she would later call for the devotion of First Saturdays; that when they pray the rosary, they should after each mystery say: "O my Jesus, forgive us, save us from the fire of hell. Lead all souls to heaven, especially those who are most in need."

The Apparitions of Our Lady: forth and fifth apparitions
These took place at Valinhos. She requested the construction of a chapel.

She concluded: "Pray, pray very much and make sacrifices for sinners; for many souls go to hell, because there are none to sacrifice themselves and to pray for them."

The Apparitions of Our Lady: sixth apparition on 13th Sept 1917

"Continue to pray the Rosary in order to obtain the end of the war. In October Our Lord will come as well as Our Lady of Dolours and Our Lady of Carmel. St Joseph will appear with the Child Jesus to bless the world. God is pleased with your sacrifices."

The Apparitions of Our Lady: seventh apparition

"I want to tell you that a chapel is to be built here in my honour. I am the Lady of the Rosary. Continue always to pray the Rosary every day."

Then the famous miracle of the sun was witnessed by 70,000 people. Lucia describes it as follows:

"Then, opening her hands, she made them reflect on the sun, and as she ascended, the reflection of her light continued to be projected on the sun itself.

"After Our Lady had disappeared into the distance of the firmament, we beheld St Joseph with the Child Jesus and Our Lady robed in white with a blue mantle, beside the sun. St Joseph and the Child appeared to bless the world, for they placed the sign of the cross with their hands.

"When a little later, this apparition disappeared, I saw Our Lord and Our Lady as Our Lady of Dolours. Our Lord appeared to bless the world in the same way as St Joseph had done.

"I saw Our Lady once more, this time resembling Our Lady of Carmel."

Later Apparitions to Lucia on 10th Dec 1925

The most Holy Virgin appeared to Lucia and by her side was the Child Jesus.

She said: "Have compassion on the Heart of your most Holy Mother, covered with thorns, with which ungrateful men pierce it at every moment, and there is no one to make an act of reparation to remove them."

On First Saturdays she said:

"Look my daughters, at my Heart, surrounded with thorns with which ungrateful men pierce me every moment by their blasphemies and you at least try to console me and say that I promise to assist at the hour of death, with the graces necessary for salvation, all those who on the first Saturday of five consecutive months, shall confess, receive Holy Communion, recite five decades of the Rosary, with the intention of making reparation for me."

Lucia had an encounter with the Child Jesus on 15th February 1926. Our Lord made the following revelations on the First Saturdays:

"It is true, my daughter, that many souls begin First Saturdays, but few finish them and those who do complete them do so in order to receive the graces that are promised thereby. It would please me more if they did five with fervour and with the intention of making reparation to the Heart of your Heavenly Mother, than if they did fifteen, in a tepid and indifferent manner."

CHAPTER 4

Judgment:
heaven, hell and purgatory

Saint Faustina's vision of heaven, hell and purgatory

Heaven

"After Holy Communion, I was carried in spirit before the throne of God. There I saw the heavenly powers which incessantly praise God. Beyond the throne I saw a brightness inaccessible to creatures, and there only the Incarnate Word enters as Mediator." (Diary 85)

"Today I was in heaven, in spirit, and I saw its inconceivable beauties and the happiness that awaits us after death. I saw how all creatures give ceaseless praise and glory to God. I saw how great is happiness in God, which spreads to all creatures, making them happy; and then all the glory and praise which springs from this happiness returns to its source; and they enter into the depths of God, contemplating the inner life of God, the Father, the Son, and the Holy Spirit, whom they will never comprehend or fathom.

"This source of happiness is unchanging in its essence, but it is always new, gushing forth happiness for all creatures. Now I understand Saint Paul who said, "eye has not seen, nor has ear heard, nor has it entered into the heart of Man what God has prepared for those who love Him." (Diary 777)

"The sight of this great majesty of God, which I came to understand more profoundly and which is worshipped by the heavenly spirits according to their degree of grace and the hierarchies into which they are divided, did not cause my soul to be stricken with terror or fear; no, no, not at all! My soul was filled with peace and love, and the more I came to know the greatness of God, the more joyful I became that He is as He is. And I rejoice immensely in

His greatness and am delighted that I am so little because, since I am little, He carries me in His arms and holds me close to His heart." (Diary 779)

"O my God, how I pity those people who do not believe in eternal life; how I pray for them that a ray of mercy would envelop them too, and that God would clasp them to His fatherly bosom." (Diary 780)

"I learned in the Heart of Jesus that in Heaven itself there is a Heaven to which not all, but only chosen souls, have access. Incomprehensible is the happiness in which the soul will be immersed. O my God, oh, that I could describe this, even in some little degree. Souls are penetrated by His divinity and pass from brightness to brightness, an unchanging light, but never monotonous, always new though never changing. O Holy Trinity, make Yourself known to souls!" (Diary 592)

"A vivid presence of God suddenly swept over me, and I was caught up in spirit before the majesty of God. I saw how the angels and the saints of the Lord give glory to God. The glory of God is so great that I dare not try to describe it, because I would not be able to do so, and souls might think that what I have written is all there is... And all that has come forth from God returns to Him in the same way and gives Him perfect glory." (Diary 1604)

Saint Faustina's vision of heaven, hell and purgatory

Hell

"Today I was led by an angel to the chasms of hell. It is a place of great torture; how awesomely large and extensive it is! The kinds of torture I saw: the first torture that constitutes hell is the loss of God; the second is perpetual remorse of conscience; the third is that one's condition will never change; the fourth is the fire that will penetrate the soul without destroying it – a terrible suffering, since it is a purely spiritual fire, lit by God's anger; the fifth torture is continual darkness and a terrible suffocating smell, and, despite the darkness, the devils and the souls of the damned see each other and all the evil, both others and their own; the sixth torture is the constant company of Satan; the seventh torture is horrible despair, hatred of God, vile words, curses and blasphemies. These are the tortures suffered by all the damned together, but that is not the end of the sufferings. There are special tortures destined for particular souls. These are the torments of the senses. Each soul undergoes terrible and indescribable sufferings, related to the manner in which it has sinned. There are caverns and pits of torture where one form of agony differs from another. I would have died at the very sight of these tortures if the omnipotence of God had not supported me. Let the sinner know that he will be tortured throughout all eternity, in those senses which he made use of to sin. I am writing this at the command of God, so that no soul may find an excuse by saying there is no hell, or that nobody has ever been there, and so no one can say what it is like.

"I, Sister Faustina, by the order of God, have visited the abysses of hell so that I might tell souls about it and testify to its existence. I cannot speak about it now; but I have received a command from God to leave it in writing. The devils were full of hatred for me, but they had to obey me at the command of God. What I have written is but a pale shadow of things I saw. But I noticed one thing: that most of the souls there are those who disbelieved that there is hell. When I came to, I could hardly recover from the fright. How terribly souls suffer there! Consequently, I pray even more fervently for the conversion of sinners. I incessantly plead God's mercy upon them. O my Jesus I would rather be in agony until the end of the world, amidst the greatest suffering, than offend You by the least sin." (Diary 741)

Saint Faustina's vision of heaven, hell and purgatory

Purgatory

"(The next night) I saw my guardian angel, who ordered me to follow him. In a moment I was in a misty place full of fire in which there was a great crowd of suffering souls. They were praying fervently, but to no avail, for themselves; only we can come to their aid. The flames which were burning them did not touch me at all.

My guardian angel did not leave me for an instant. I asked these souls what their greatest suffering was. They answered me in one voice that their greatest torment was longing for God. I saw Our Lady visiting the souls in purgatory. The souls call her "The Star of the Sea". She brings them refreshment. I wanted to talk with them some more, but my guardian angel beckoned me to leave. We went out of that prison of suffering. (I heard an interior voice) which said, **"My mercy does not want this, but justice demands it."** Since that time, I am in closer communion with the suffering souls." (Diary 20)

"Once I was summoned to the judgment (seat) of God. I stood alone before the Lord. Jesus appeared such as we know Him during His Passion. After a moment, His wounds disappeared except for five, those in His hands, His feet and His side. Suddenly I saw the complete condition of my soul as God sees it. I could clearly see all that is displeasing to God. I did not know that even the smallest transgressions will have to be accounted for. What a moment! Who can describe it? To stand before the Thrice-Holy God! Jesus asked me, **"Who are you?"** I answered "I am your servant, Lord." **"You are guilty of one day of fire in purgatory."** I wanted to throw myself immediately into the flames of purgatory, but Jesus stopped me and said, **"Which do you prefer, suffer now for one day in purgatory or for a short while on Earth?"** I replied, "Jesus, I want to suffer in purgatory, and I want to suffer also the greatest pains on Earth, even if it were to the end of the world." Jesus said, **"One (of the two) is enough; you will go back to Earth, and there you will suffer much, but not for long; you will accomplish My will and My desires, and a faithful servant of Mine will help you to do this. Now, rest your head on My bosom, on My heart, and draw from it strength and power for these sufferings, because you will find neither relief nor help nor comfort anywhere else. Know that you will have much, much to suffer, but don't let this frighten you; I am with you."** (Diary 36)

"One evening, one of the deceased sisters, who had already visited me a few times, appeared to me. The first time I had seen her, she had been in great suffering, and then gradually these sufferings had diminished; this time she was radiant with happiness, and she told me she was already in heaven…And further, as a sign that she only now was in heaven, God would bless our house. Then she came closer to me, embraced me sincerely and said, "I must go now." I understood how closely the three stages of a soul's life are bound together; that is to say, life on Earth, in purgatory and in Heaven (the Communion of Saints)." (Diary 594)

"After Vespers today, there was a procession to the cemetery. I could not go, because I was on duty at the gate. But that did not stop me at all from praying for the souls. As the procession was returning from the cemetery to the chapel, my soul felt the presence of many souls. I understood the great justice of God, how each one had to pay off the debt to the last cent." (Diary 1375)

"One day, I saw two roads. One was broad, covered with sand and flowers, full of joy, music and all sorts of pleasures. People walked along it, dancing and enjoying themselves. They reached the end without realising it. And at the end of the road there was a horrible precipice; that is, the abyss of hell. The souls fell blindly into it; as they walked, so they fell. And their number was so great that it was impossible to count them. And I saw the other road, or rather, a path, for it was narrow and strewn with thorns and rocks; and the people who walked along it had tears in their eyes, and all kinds of suffering befell them. Some fell down upon the rocks, but stood up immediately and went on. At the end of the road there was a magnificent garden filled with all sorts of happiness, and all these souls entered there. At the very first instant they forgot all their sufferings." (Diary 153)

Reflections on judgment

According to the teaching of the Catholic Church, between heaven, where all souls who die may enter into eternal bliss, and hell where souls may go and suffer eternal torment, there is a middle destination which is called purgatory where souls may go and suffer temporal punishment or purification. Souls who go to purgatory may have committed venial sins which they have not expiated or they may have committed mortal sins which may have been forgiven after confession. These souls may need to undergo temporal punishment because they may still have stains which they need to remove. Temporal punishments may be remitted in proportion to the contrition expressed through prayers and actions of the sinner. It is important that if there are still any stains remaining after the expression of contrition, they should be atoned for in this world by penance. This is because unremitted temporal punishment and stains of venial sin constitute defilement of the soul in the sight of God. Christ refers to His justice and mercy. The explanation for this is that God's nature hates injustices in a person. God is so holy that sin and injustices cannot cross His path, He who has a profound and keen knowledge of our souls and is infinitely holy.

Even though souls in purgatory can no longer do any penance for their sins to enable them to reach heaven, the faithful on Earth can pray for them to obtain relief. This can be done through prayers and sacrifices such as almsgiving, acts of mortification and, most importantly, celebration of holy masses. These are important instruments of mercy that may appease God's justice. There are also practical devotions instituted by the Church which may be offered for the release of the souls from the prison of purgatory. Another important help enjoyed by souls in purgatory is the communion of saints. Christ, who is the head of the Church, is at the same time the second person of the Holy Trinity. In his own mercy, he has allowed the faithful on Earth to make prayers and sacrifices to Him for the release of the suffering souls in purgatory. Also, as we are told by Sister Faustina, the Blessed Virgin Mary is the help of the suffering souls in purgatory. Through the prayers and sacrifices of the faithful, she can use these treasures of the Church to help the suffering souls in purgatory. The saints can no longer do penance to obtain relief for souls in purgatory. However, the faithful on Earth can pray through them to intercede for Holy Souls in purgatory.

It is very important that humanity should see purgatory as an act of Divine Mercy. The existence of purgatory should inspire in the faithful a holy fear of God which will lead us to seek only His glory and constantly meditate on the truth that every stain of sin offends his justice and glory. Further, holy fear should save us from hell, eternal damnation and separation from our Creator. Such a spiritual disposition should help all souls to perform holy actions that could expiate our sins before death.

Saint Catherine of Siena entreated all God's people to remember that God, by the blood of Christ, has brought us forgiveness of our sins and will do everything to protect us from the Devil and his agents. She said God has given us enough graces to overcome evil and that we can never be constrained by the Devil to commit sin. This means that we have the free will aided by God's grace to overcome sin. She believed that by remembering the sacrifices of Christ, souls will be disposed to love Him and that the affection for Christ will help us to await God's judgement with joy.

It is salutary when Saint Faustina reveals in the diary that even in purgatory Divine Mercy is active. She discloses that in purgatory, our will is united with God's will and therefore we have full awareness of God's justice and that souls in purgatory would themselves reject Heaven if their stains were not removed. Such awareness should inspire us to self-knowledge, which constantly brings us to the awareness of our own sins and ingratitude towards God's mercy.

Hell and Damnation

Christ's earthly sacrifice and redemptive work should convince us that He wants no soul to be condemned to eternal death. This means that souls who are damned deliberately rejected God's mercy. Such souls did not care about what would happen to them after this life. In effect, they leave this world with a hatred of Christ, their Redeemer and decide to join the Devil, the enemy of God. Through the Divine Mercy, Christ calls all those who are in danger of damnation to return to God.

Also, in His mercy, God has allowed some mystics like Saint Teresa of Avila, Saint Catherine of Siena and Saint Faustina to have visions of the three states of humans after this life.

Saint Catherine has provided insights into what happens to souls after death. She reveals that the peace of the just man's death is greater or less according to the perfection of his soul. The more their will is united to God, the less they suffer. She says that during their lifetimes the just men have already waged war against the world, the Devil and their own flesh. So when they come to the point of death, just souls die peacefully because they have conquered their spiritual enemies during their lifetime. Saint Catherine says that the bodily senses of just people cannot accuse them because they have overcome the body with penance, humility, prayer and good works. On her part, Saint Faustina advises that souls should constantly examine their consciences and express contrition for their sins as well as asking the Blessed Virgin Mary to intercede for them. They should also put their trust in the Blood of Christ, not in their own merits. In doing so, according to the saint, the Devil is rendered powerless when he tries to frighten them after death. They keep away and their threats do the souls no harm. The saint says the mind of the soul illuminated by holy faith is drawn by God to Himself by the merits of Jesus Christ.

Saint Catherine has advice for sinners. She reveals that the Devil accuses sinners immediately after their death and tries to disturb the conscience of their souls for having been unfaithful to their Creator. She says if the Devil is able to make the soul feel powerless through despair, they are rendered powerless. She therefore advises souls not only to express contrition for their sins in this life but also to appeal to the Divine Mercy. The soul obtains Divine Mercy in the following way: a) sinners should express remorse through recognizing their sins and unloading their conscience through a good confession. b) Through contrition and repentance, the soul obtains the Divine Mercy to overcome the Devil after death.

Saint Catherine makes a distinction between a false repentance and a true repentance. She describes a false repentance as the situation where the person is sorry only because he might go to hell and lose God but not because of the offence and ingratitude towards God, who is holy and who sent His Son to redeem us. True repentance, therefore, is where the sinner is sorry and repents for the offence against God, who is holy and who has given us life and all the gifts of salvation. Again, according to Saint Catherine, all souls must focus on God's mercy and believe that repentance is at their disposal, even at the point of death. They should never despair that they have sinned to a point where Divine Mercy is not available. The attitude of despair is dangerous because it would allow the Devil to throw them into confusion after death. Trust in Divine Mercy is therefore the greatest gift flowing from God to mankind through the heart of Jesus. It is the greatest weapon that helps the soul at the hour of death.

Christ to Saint Faustina:

"Write this: before I come as the Just Judge, I am coming first as the King of Mercy. Before the day of justice arrives, there will be given to people a sign in the heavens of this sort.

"All light in the heavens will be extinguished, and there will be great darkness over the whole earth. Then the sign of the cross will be seen in the sky, and from the openings where the hands and the feet of the Saviour were nailed will come forth great lights which will light up the Earth for a period of time. This will take place shortly before the last day." (Diary 83)

Saint Faustina wrote down the above messages, which were revealed to her by Christ. They refer to the signs that would be visible in the heavens just before the Last Judgment.

In the Church's document known as the *Constitution on the Church of the Second Vatican Council*, the Church affirms that humanity is called upon to be faithful to God and that they will achieve their full perfection only if they are perfectly united to Christ; that Christ came to establish the Last Times, meaning that the promised restoration of sinful humanity which God promised in the Old Testament began in Christ through the Holy Spirit. Through faith in Christ and especially His teachings, we are told of the meaning of our temporal life and the way to obey God's commandments in order to attain perfection in the glory of heaven.

So the final judgement referred to in the revelations to Saint Faustina is the day when the full consequences of our salvation will be revealed.

The cross which, according to Christ's revelation to Saint Faustina, will be seen in the sky renews our confidence in God's power and glory. Through Christ's suffering on the cross, we are shown God's power in weakness and the fact that it was through the cross that our salvation was accomplished. The cross is further associated with God's victory over Satan and his unrepentant sinners who are God's rebels. The illumination of the cross will have different meanings depending on whether or not we have obeyed God's call to redemption. On the Day of Judgment, sinners will see in the illumination of the cross, their negligence and faults and the fact that they have been responsible for their own damnation. Even in their damnation, they will appreciate God's justice. On the other hand, those who have obeyed God's call will realise the fruits of their co-operation with the humanity and divinity of Christ. They will rejoice and see that their redemption is at hand because they fully embraced the cross. They will realise that the work of salvation has been accomplished. It will be the fulfilment of their "Credo".

The reference to Saint Faustina by Christ about total darkness in the world confirms the gospel story of the end of the world: "There will be signs in the sun, the moon, and the stars. On the Earth, nations will be in anguish, distraught at the roaring of the sea and the waves. Men will die of fright in anticipation of what is coming upon the earth. The powers in the heavens will be shaken. After that, men will see the Son of Man coming on a cloud with great power and glory."(Luke 25-27)

Christ now declares a period of mercy based on God's love for mankind because Christ's work of salvation has pleased Him. We are all called upon to respond to this mercy individually and collectively. So as to benefit greatly from God's mercy, we should renounce the modern culture of atheism and rejection of God and His commandments, false prosperity, the institution of sinful moralities based on lust. We are called to our true nature, which is found through obedience to God's commandments.

PART 2

Responding to God's Mercy

CHAPTER 1

The Great Retreat Conducted by Christ

Reflections on the retreat conducted by Our Lord Jesus Christ

The Circumstances of the Retreat

In the year of her death (5th October 1938), St Faustina was ordered by Our Lord Jesus Christ to attend a three-day retreat conducted by Himself. The retreat took place on the three days preceding Pentecost. Our Lord gave to St Faustina certain spiritual subjects to reflect on. These subjects were intended to elevate the soul to a higher degree of perfection and also to serve as means of Christian perfection to all pilgrim souls here on earth.

Our Lord Himself conceded that the retreat was an exceptional event and, indeed, a special privilege for the Saint. "**The graces that are not given to other souls to discern, not even from a distance, nourish you every day, like the daily bread.**" (Diary 1753)

As the Saint was commanded by Our Lord to write the diary, it is obviously His intention that all souls would benefit from a careful reflection on the spiritual matters that Our Lord raised during the retreat. They must be considered as addressed to all pilgrim souls.

First Day of the Retreat

Subjects of Meditation

1   Christ to St Faustina: "**Consider My daughter, Who it is to whom your heart is so closely united by the vows. Before I made the world, I loved you with the love your heart is experiencing today and, throughout the centuries. My love will never change.**" (Diary 1754)

Reflections

The words of Our Lord invite the people of God to reflect constantly on the attributes, the nature and character of God. To meditate and contemplate the attributes of God is to make us tremble about what He offers us in return for our little sacrifices of love. He is a God who is holy, loving and merciful and who calls us to join Him to share His extraordinary attributes.

Christ is also offering us free gifts founded in unconditional love which should bring us to perfection. He calls us to meditate on and appreciate our individual vocations, our baptismal and any other vows that we make to God according to our own state in life. Saint Faustina reveals the impact made on herself by the words of Christ as follows: "Burning with an inner fire of love, I went out to the garden to cool off; when I looked up at the heavens, a new flame of love flooded my heart." (Diary 1755) She later writes: "What a paradise it is for a soul when the heart knows itself to be so loved by God."(Diary 1756)

2   Christ to St Faustina: **"Today, you will read chapter fifteen of the Gospel of Saint John."** (Diary 1757)

Chapter 15 of St John's Gospel

The True Vine

"I am the true vine, and My Father is the vinedresser. Every branch in me that bears no fruit He cuts away, and every branch that does bear fruit he prunes to make it bear even more. You are clean already, by means of the word that I have spoken to you. Remain in Me, as I in you. As a branch cannot bear fruit all by itself, unless it remains part of the vine, neither can you unless you remain in Me. I am the vine, you are the branches. Whoever remains in Me, with Me in Him, bear a fruit in plenty; for cut off from Me you can do nothing. Anyone who does not remain in Me is thrown away like a branch – and withers; these branches are collected and thrown on the fire and are burnt. If you remain in Me and My words remain in you, you may ask for whatever you please and you will get it. It is to the glory of My Father that you should bear much fruit and be My disciples. I have loved you just as the Father has loved Me. Remain in My love. If you keep My commandments you will remain in My love. Just as I have kept My Father's commandments and remain in his love. I have told you this so that My own joy may be in you and your joy be complete. This is My commandment: love one another as I have loved you. No one can have greater love than to lay down his life for his friends. You are My friends, if you do what I command you. I shall no longer call you servants, because a servant does not know his master's business; I call you friends, because I have made known to you everything I have learnt from My Father. You did not choose Me, no, I chose you; and I commissioned you to go out and to bear fruit, fruit that will last; so that the Father will give you anything you ask him in My name. My command to you is love one another.

"If the world hates you, you must realize that it hated Me before it hated you. If you belonged to the world, the world would love you as its own; but because you do not belong to the world, because My choice of you has drawn you out of the world, that is why the world hates you. Remember the words I said to you: A servant is not greater than his master. If they persecuted Me, they will persecute you too; if they kept my word, they will keep yours as well. But it will be on my account that they will do all this to you, because they do not know the One who sent me. If I had not come, if I had not spoken to them, they would have been blameless; but as it is they have no excuse for their sin. Anyone who hates Me hates My Father. If I had not performed such works among them as no one else has ever done, they would be blameless; but as it is, in spite of what they have seen, they hate both Me and My Father. But all this was only to fulfil the words written in their Law: 'They hated me without reason'. When the Paraclete comes, whom I shall send to you from the Father, the Spirit of truth who issues from the Father, He will be My witness. And you too will be witnesses, because you have been with Me from the beginning."

Reflections on Chapter 15 of St John's Gospel

1   Jesus announces His departure from His community but
    as He promised before His ascension, He would be with
    them until the end of time. Because of His eternal sacrifice
    on the cross, the Father would continue to distribute gifts
    to the community through the Holy Spirit.

2   Through the Eucharist, Christ is present in the
    faithful. In this way, He brings the believer into a new
    relationship with the Father. Christ then is present in the
    faith community as He promised.

3   The gifts generated by the Spirit will strengthen them
    during future persecutions but they must constantly keep
    in mind His own sacrifices so as to continue to proclaim
    His death in this life.

4   The Holy Spirit, the Paraclete will help them to
    understand all the messages He has sent to the world
    through His disciples. The Paraclete will not bring any
    new teaching that is independent of what Christ had
    revealed. Through the Spirit, they will receive strength
    and understanding to enable them to do good works for
    the glory of the new kingdom.

5   By His resurrection, Christ has overcome Satan and his
    agents. If He was humiliated and crucified, it does not
    signal victory for Satan. It is only a sign of His obedience
    to His Father. By the Father's will, the cross which signifies
    total humility has overcome the pride of Satan. Humility
    and lowliness therefore acquire new spiritual meanings.

Christ uses the imagery of the vine to remind all His followers
the necessity of remaining with Him. By the Father's decree, all His
plans of salvation were to be accomplished by the life and death of
Christ, His only Son. Just as He created the universe through Christ
and for Christ, the whole mankind and indeed the universe would
only be rescued from its misery through Christ. God would only
reveal Himself and His mysteries only to those who through faith

are prepared to share the mysteries of Christ. Again through Christ, believers are helped by the gifts of the Holy Spirit to overcome sins.

The imagery of the vine can also be explained by the manner that the Father made Christ accomplish His saving plan. Christ's assumed nature was joined to His divinity so that by imitating this human-divine nature of Christ, mankind would be enabled to overcome sin and enter into the mysteries of salvation. This union with Christ's nature enables the Holy Spirit to work in us, to bear fruit. It is only in this way that we can pass from mortality to immortality and be united with God the Father. This is why St Paul says that Christ is the key that opens all the hidden treasures of God's wisdom and knowledge. This is because it is only through Christ that we have access in one Spirit to the Father. The vine imagery then teaches us that as individual christians and as the one people of God, we are all nourished in the One Body of Christ in the unity of the Holy Spirit and peform good works in accordance with the gifts of the Holy Spirit.

All christians are reminded therefore that their perfection can only be achieved through imitating Christ and rejecting the world of erroneous doctrines and moralities. Through their fidelity to Christ, christians are able to represent Jesus in the world and with Him glorify His Father.

If Christ says that the disciples have become His friends, it is because they are prepared to imitate Him even unto death. Sacrifice therefore becomes the foundation of the new kingdom of God and makes all who believe in the gospel, the adopted sons of God. Through sacrifice and suffering, Christians are able to bear fruit and reach their true end which is their Father in heaven. Christ's death and resurrection confirm that Christ through suffering has overthrown the kingdom of satan and his followers in a sinful world.

Christ to Saint Faustina: **"My daughter; consider the life of God which is found in the Church for the salvation and the** sanctification of your soul. Consider the use that you make of these treasures of grace, of these efforts of My love." (Diary 1758)

Reflections

St Thomas Aquinas offers us great help in understanding the subject of imitating the life, death and resurrection of Christ, especially the meaning of his suffering. These words are taken from the conferences of the saint. The passage goes as follows:

"In the passion of Christ we find a remedy for all the evils which come upon us on account of our sins. But the passion is not less useful to us as an example. Indeed the passion of Christ is sufficient in itself to instruct us completely in our whole life. For if anyone wants to live a perfect life, he has only to despise the things that Christ despised on the cross, and to desire what Christ desired. The cross provides an example of every virtue.

"If you are looking for an example of charity, 'Greater love has no man than this, that a man lay down his life for his friends.' This was what Christ did on the cross. If He gave up His life for us, it ought not to be a burden for us to put up with every evil, whatever it be, for His sake.

"If you are looking for patience, you will find it in its highest form on the cross. The greatness of patience is measured by two things, either when someone puts up patiently with grievous things, or when he suffers things which he could have evaded but did not. Christ suffered greatly and with patience on the cross: 'when He suffered, He did not threaten; like a lamb that is led to the slaughter, He opened not his mouth.' That is how great was the patience of Christ on the cross: 'Let us run with perseverance the race that is set before us, looking to Jesus, the pioneer and perfecter of our faith, Who for the joy that was set before Him, endured the cross, despising the shame.'

"If you are looking for an example of humility, look at the cross. There, God willed to be judged by Pontius Pilate and to die.

"If you are looking for an example of obedience, follow Him who was obedient to the Father, even unto death. 'For as by one man's disobedience, many were made sinners, so by one man's obedience many will be made righteous.'

"If you are looking for a model of contempt for earthly things, follow Him Who is the 'King of kings, and Lord of lords...in Whom are hid all the treasures of wisdom and knowledge.' He was naked on the cross, derided and spat upon, struck and crowned with thorns, and finally given vinegar to drink. Do not, then, be attached to fine clothes and riches, for 'they divided My garments among them.' Do not seek for honours, for He knew mockery and beating. Do not seek honourable rank, because 'they plaited a crown of thorns and placed it on My head'. Do not seek after fine foods, because 'for My thirst, they gave Me vinegar to drink.'"

The Saint's sanctification and salvation can only be attained in the Church, the Body of Christ. Note that the stray sheep must be brought back to join the rest of the flock.

Christ has suffered to obtain many graces for the Church and humanity. Many do not bother to reflect on the cost of our redemption because of the attractions of this world which darken minds.
Others receive gifts which they fail to use to achieve higher degrees of perfection, for God's glory and sanctification of others.

We do not even consider the power and majesty of the giver. From St John's passage, Christ says He lives in us and we in Him but we do not reflect on this. We become His living members if we have the proper spiritual disposition and are ready to do His will.

St Columban advises as follows: "Therefore seek the supreme wisdom, not by verbal debate, but by the perfection of a good life, not with the tongue but with faith which issues from singleness of heart, not with that which is gathered from the guess of a learned irreligion."

When St Faustina enters into "profound recollection" of her vows, she clearly sees the attributes of God.

She sees beyond the form and signs and is then able to see the spiritual realities and put the gifts to use.

Conference on Spiritual Warfare

Christ to Saint Faustina:**"My daughter, I want to teach you about spiritual warfare. Never trust in yourself but abandon yourself totally to My will. In desolation, darkness and various doubts, have recourse to Me and to your spiritual director. He will always answer you in My name. Do not bargain with any temptation; lock yourself immediately in My Heart and, at the first opportunity, reveal the temptation to the confessor. Put your self-love in the last place, so that it does not taint your deeds. Bear with yourself with great patience. Do not neglect interior mortifications. Always justify to yourself the opinions of your superiors and of your confessor. Shun murmurers like a plague. Let all act as they like; you are to act as I want you to.**

"Observe the rule as faithfully as you can. If someone causes you trouble, think what good you can do for the person who caused you to suffer. Do not pour out your feelings. Be silent when you are rebuked. Do not ask everyone's opinion but only the opinion of your confessor; be as frank and simple as a child with him. Do not become discouraged by ingratitude. Do not examine with curiosity the roads down which I lead you. When boredom and discouragement beat against your heart, run away from yourself and hide in My heart. Do not

fear struggle; courage itself often intimidates temptations, and they dare not attack us.

"Always fight with the deep conviction that I am with you. Do not be guided by feeling, because it is not always under your control; but all merit lies in the will. Always depend upon your superiors, even in the smallest things. I will not delude you with prospects of peace and consolations; on the contrary, prepare for great battles. Know that you are now on a great stage where all Heaven and Earth are watching you. Fight like a knight, so that I can reward you. Do not be unduly fearful, because you are not alone." (Diary 1760)

Reflections on the words of Christ

On the Nature of our Spiritual Enemies

On the matter of our spiritual enemy, Christ permitted Saint Faustina to have an encounter with Satan and, through her, to instruct us how we should deal with evil temptations that may occur to us on different spiritual levels. Saint Faustina describes her experience as follows:

"Total discouragement came over me. Then I heard Satan's voice: 'See how contradictory everything is that Jesus gives to you: He tells you to found a convent, and then He gives you sickness; He tells you to set about establishing this Feast of Mercy while the whole world does not at all want such a feast. Why do you pray for this feast? It is so inopportune.' My soul remained silent and, by an act of will, continued to pray without entering into conversation with the Spirit of Darkness. Nevertheless, such an extraordinary disgust with life came over me that I had to make a great act of the will to consent to go on living.

"And again I heard the tempter's words: 'Ask for death for yourself, tomorrow after Holy Communion. God will hear you, for He has heard you so many times before and has given you that which you asked of Him.'

"I remained silent and, by an act of will, I began to pray, or rather, submitted myself to God, asking Him interiorly not to abandon me at this moment. It was already eleven o'clock at night, and there was silence all around. The sisters were all asleep in their cells, and my soul alone was struggling with great exertion.

"The tempter went on: 'Why should you bother about other souls? You ought to be praying only for yourself. As for sinners, they will be converted without your prayers. I see that you are suffering very much at this moment. I'm going to give you a piece of advice on which your happiness will depend: Never speak about God's mercy and, in particular do not encourage sinners to trust in God's mercy, because they deserve a just punishment. Another very important thing: Do not tell your confessors, and especially this extraordinary confessor and the priest in Vilnius, about what goes on in your soul. I know them; I know who they are, and so I want to put you on your guard against them. You see, to live as a good nun, it is sufficient to live like all the others. Why expose yourself to so many difficulties?'

"I remained silent, and by an act of will I dwelt in God, although a moan escaped from my heart. Finally, the tempter went away and I, exhausted, fell asleep immediately." (Diary 1497-1498)

Christ uses the above incident to show us that Saint Faustina was triumphant over Satan because she united herself to His own triumph on the cross. Christ, our shepherd and teacher, strengthens and guides us through the Spirit. After Saint Faustina's encounter, Christ immediately comes to her and states as follows: **"Satan gained nothing by tempting you, because you did not enter into conversation with him. Continue to act in this way. You gave Me great glory today by fighting so faithfully. Let it be confirmed and engraved on your heart that I am always with you, even if you don't feel My presence at the time of battle."** (Diary 1499)

St Paul warns us that we are engaged in warfare with principalities that we cannot see. Christ is instructing us as to how we should react to these spiritual enemies who try to influence our senses.

The greatest weapon against them is not to rely on our own

wisdom but to trust in God's protection. Christ reveals that He uses others, like our Spiritual Directors, to guide us. We are to take note of this during our own trials and tribulations because God uses holy people to guide us in all circumstances of life.

Another protective shield is mortification, which is our own way of renouncing the world and its attractions, and human respect that makes us sensitive to the world instead of to God's will. In this Christ calls for simple trust in God. It is assuring when Christ reveals that heaven takes keen interest in the way we deal with our trials and temptations. He reveals to Saint Faustina that on such occasions, we are on a stage where the whole of heaven is watching us. Did Christ not say in the gospel that the whole of heaven rejoices over the repentance of a sinner? Christ reveals that the whole court of Heaven rejoices whenever we overcome the trials and temptations of this world.

St Teresa of Avila has something to say on spiritual warfare. She explains that without the Devil's temptations, souls on the way to perfection would only enjoy God's consolations and would therefore become complacent. The soul would also be deprived of all occasions of merit. "When a soul is continuously in a condition of this kind I do not consider it at all safe, nor do I think it possible for the Spirit of the Lord to remain in a soul continuously in this way during our life of exile." (*Interior Castle* 230)

St Teresa adds that, when through God's mercy the soul manages to overcome the state where he gradually renounces worldly affairs, honours, ambitions and negative influences on the senses, "the Devil makes terrible assaults upon the soul by endeavouring to show the soul the thing of the world and they pretend that earthly pleasures are almost eternal; they remind the soul of the esteem in which it is held in the world, of its friends and relatives, of the way in which its health will be endangered by penances."

On Those who Cause us Suffering
Christ encourages us to bear all sufferings that may even come from persons who we deem to be leading holy lives. St Faustina

gives us an example in her diary (31). In a vision, she saw a big crowd of people in the convent chapel. The crowd included the sisters of the convent, a large congregation and even members of her family. St Faustina narrates that a voice told her that she was to occupy a prominent place on the altar but that as soon as she left to go to the altar, many persons, including nuns and members of her family began to throw mud, sand, stones and other missiles at her. Encouraged by the voice, she persevered and took her place on the altar. Once she occupied her prominent place, she saw that the same people who had frustrated her journey by throwing missiles at her were now asking her for graces. She said she then occupied a position of ineffable happiness and was in a position to distribute graces as she wished.

The vision revealed to Saint Faustina is an encouragement to all faithful Christians who have been called to participate in Christ's redemptive work to foresee the future fruits of their good works for souls. "Do not be guided by feeling because it is not always under your control; but all merit lies in the will." The words of a holy person, Diadochus of Photike, will perhaps help us to understand the admonition of Christ, stated above. "Indeed those who struggle must ceaselessly maintain calmness of thought: thus the mind will be able to discriminate between the suggestions which pass through it and will place those which are good and come from God in the treasure house of memory, while it will eject from this natural reservoir those which are evil and come from the Devil."

On Christ's Warning to Saint Faustina about the Dangers of Self-love

Self-love refers to a disordered love of self, with the object of seeking one's own personal good without considering God's will and plan of salvation. Self-love therefore goes against divine charity because man should first and foremost respond to God's love. The Catechism tells us that God created us to know, love and serve Him.

When Moses was called by God's love to serve Him, he realized that he had two choices: either to love God and denounce

80

the sinful disobedience of his people or to be faithful to God and divine sanctity. Similarly, in the scripture account of Christ's temptation by the Devil, we are offered two distinct images, one image of renunciation of the Devil's ways and another image of sacrifice and renunciation of the world so as to be able to love God. Unlike self-love, true charity and love of God mean repentance and rejection of the Devil. True love therefore means man's acceptance of his supernatural destiny in God and total rejection of all material attractions.

On the question of self-love, Saint Bonaventure gives an account of the rebel angels who fell from God's grace into damnation. He describes these angels as having the living images and perfections of God, with wisdom and true knowledge. However, Lucifer and these angels became dazzled by their own perfections and committed the sin of self-idolatry. They therefore rebelled against God and fell by their own pride. They were therefore in rebellion against God's love.

When we are in the state of pure love of God, we are fully prepared in love for a definitive encounter with God who is love. Self-love is therefore annihilated because of our love of God and neighbour which brings about in us a deeper understanding of God's love, a new life in which God speaks and acts in us. In truly loving our brothers and sisters, we love the Lord Himself and we become the true children of our Father who is in Heaven.

Saint Gertrude considers the question of self-love as follows: "You did teach me also, that the great perfection of the soul consists in relinquishing the pleasure which it finds in the affections, in order to occupy itself, for the love of You, in watching over its exterior senses, and in labouring in works of charity for the salvation of its neighbour." Our Lord revealed to the saint that when He enters into a soul by the Holy Sacrament of the Eucharist, He takes over the desire and will of the soul and He presents the desire and will of the soul so formed to His Father, to obtain from Him the graces which this soul needs. The Saint therefore concludes that through renunciation of self, the soul receives a pure light from God which enables it to perform works of charity efficaciously.

God's Use of Faithful Souls (expiatory sacrifices)

Through His own sacrifices, Christ teaches us that God merits being served and loved at whatever cost. However, by His resurrection, He also teaches us that these sacrifices lead to indescribable glory. At the Transfiguration, the three faithful disciples, Peter, James and John, were enabled to see the glorious part of Christ as contrasted with His poor earthly image of patience and suffering. We can say the same of a soul that is faithful to God's will. These souls are spiritually gifted with the unction of the Holy Spirit which confers on them graces to enable them to do good works and continue to acquire merits that will bring them glory in heaven. They have immense glory and special supernatural light for eternity and are therefore able even to do heroic works because they have intimate union with Christ who communicates to them His own will and merits. The true imitation of Christ therefore snatches us away from all spiritual dangers.

St Teresa of Avila describes the dignity of a faithful soul as follows: "The soul of the righteous man is nothing but a paradise." She said that such souls have a great capacity to be made perfect and that God dwells in such souls. "Secret things pass between the soul and God." Saint Teresa saw that God manifests favours to certain souls to enable them to understand the value of the soul and the treasures laid up for the soul and to encourage perfection in other souls.

It can therefore be said that all souls who submit to God's will receive appropriate spiritual merits and returns because they become a model of God's own integrity. He will continue to guide all such persons to Himself because His own Spirit is planted in their hearts. Many divine secrets that are hidden from the great and the wise are revealed by God to souls that totally submit themselves to Him.

Second Day of Christ's directed retreat

"My daughter, today consider My Sorrowful Passion in all its immensity. Consider it as if it had been undertaken for your sake alone." (Diary 1761)

Reflections

What is significant about the works of Christ is the impact that they make on Saint Faustina interiorly. The Saint had an interior vision of the inestimable value of the human soul and the great damage that sin does to the soul. Saint Faustina then appreciated the need to suffer in order to be in a state to rescue sinful souls, especially those at the point of death, so that they could receive God's mercy. The Saint understood that mercy for sinful souls had been made possible because of the immense merits of Christ's sorrowful passion.

Saint Teresa of Avila also gives an insight into the spiritual damage that sin causes the soul. Saint Teresa described the soul as being like a tree: it is planted in God, who is the sole source of living water, but it becomes hideous through sin. She added that God is at the centre of our soul but is unable to help the soul when it is in a state of sin. She said sinful actions lead to darkness and spiritual destruction because sinful actions are not rooted in God. On the other hand, the works of a soul in grace please God, who is able to provide them with all the graces needed for perfection.

In her revelation regarding the condition of a soul in mortal sin, St Teresa of Avila, in her book called The *Interior Castle*, revealed the following: "No thicker darkness exists, and there is nothing dark and black which is not much less than this."

Saint Faustina noted in her diary that she had a vision of how horrible sinful souls are in the sight of God. She asked God how He was able to endure such a terrible sight, to which God replied that time is on His side.

In the above words that Christ uttered to Saint Faustina, He is asking all souls to understand why He needed to undergo His Passion to appease the offences that souls cause to God. If souls embark on this contemplation of Christ's Passion, they will be able to endure their own suffering and to join their sacrifices with Him to expiate the sins of the world before the throne of His Father.

Christ to Saint Faustina: **"My daughter, consider the rule and the vows which you have offered to Me. You know how highly**

I value them; all the graces that I have for the souls of religious are connected with the rule and the vows."(Diary 1763)

The words of Christ specifically refer to the rule and vows made by the religious. However, we may also refer them generally to all the vows and promises that all the people of God make to their Creator. For example, during baptism, all baptized persons make a vow to renounce Satan and all the ways of the world. God takes on board all these vows for His own glory and at the end of our lives, we will have to answer whether the vows were used for our benefit and the benefit of other souls. Let us see how this vow is expressed in Psalm 116:

> What return can I make to Yahweh
> for his generosity to me?
> I shall take up the cup of salvation
> and call on the name of Yahweh.
> I shall fulfil my vows to Yahweh,
> witnessed by all his people.
> (Psalm 116:12-14)

The Psalmist is making his vows to God for his mercies and has pledged to keep his vow. Solomon speaks of promises made to God as follows: "If you make a vow to God, discharge it without delay, for God has no love for fools. Discharge your vow. Better a vow unmade than made and not discharged." (Ecclesiastes: 4-5). So the message is that a vow is voluntary, but after we make it, we are committed to keep it. Vows and promises to God take on a more serious dimension when we see that Christ observed all human laws that did not bind Him because of his obedience to the Father. He was indeed prepared to suffer the humiliation of death on the cross to fulfil his vows to the Father. With our baptism, we are set apart through our vows to accomplish God's purposes. Before taking vows, we should have been aware of the dangers and obstacles that the vows involve. We should be prepared to endure insults, dishonour and spiritual attacks but be resolved to trust God to give us the strength to overcome our weaknesses.

Saint Paul, reflecting on the matter of responding to God's call, stated as follows: "He who had set me apart from the day of my birth, and called me by His grace, saw fit to make His son known in me so that I could preach His gospel among gentiles." (Gal. 15) Here Saint Paul implies that we make vows when we respond to God's call for purposes pre-ordained by Him. There should be therefore no human or spiritual obstacle to God's call because He makes sure that He provides the graces adequate for us to fulfil the vow.

Saint Paul, referring to his own call, said: "My first thought was not to hold any consultations with any human creature; I did not go up to Jerusalem to see those who had been apostles longer than myself." Saint Paul's message is that God addresses calls to individuals for reasons known to Himself and no individuals or events should come between our call and God.

Christ to Saint Faustina: **"Today, My daughter, for your reading, you shall take chapter nineteen of Saint John's Gospel, and read it, not only with your lips, but with your heart."** (Diary 1765)

Chapter Nineteen of St John's Gospel

"Pilate then had Jesus taken away and scourged; and after this, the soldiers twisted some thorns into a crown and put it on His head and dressed Him in a purple robe. They kept coming up to Him and saying, 'Hail, king of the Jews!' and slapping him in the face.

"Pilate came outside again and said to them, 'Look, I am going to bring Him out to you to let you see that I find no case against Him.' Jesus then came out wearing the crown of thorns and the purple robe. Pilate said, 'Here is the man.' When they saw Him, the chief priests and the guards shouted, 'Crucify Him! Crucify Him!' Pilate said, 'Take Him yourselves and crucify Him: I find no case against Him.' The Jews replied, 'We have a Law, and according to that Law He ought to be put to death, because He has claimed to be Son of God.'

"When Pilate heard them say this, his fears increased. Re-entering the Praetorium, he said to Jesus, 'Where do You come from?' But Jesus made no answer. Pilate then said to Him, 'Are you refusing to speak to me? Surely You know I have power to release You and I have power to crucify You.' Jesus replied, 'You would have no power over Me at all if it had not been given you from above; that is why the man who handed Me over to you has the greater guilt.'" (John 19)

The Passion Narrative

Reflections

Jesus is flogged like a crucified prisoner crowned with thorns and mocked as a king. Pilate claims to have found nothing for which to condemn Jesus and shows Him to the people, with the comment "Look, the man!" The justice of this world is thus condemned in the process because Jesus has been beaten and is attired in the crown and robe. The wretched victim Christ, a true friend of the helpless world, becomes the prototype of the new kingdom. The old world is condemned by its own form of justice. Satan and his followers have given God the tool of justice to condemn them to eternal ruin. Ironically, in His earthly wretchedness, Jesus is crowned the new king. The Jews specify the charge that according to their law Jesus ought to die for making Himself 'Son of God' The centurion indeed confirms this and proclaims Him the son of God after His death; The error of the Jews is they have crucified an innocent king.

Jesus' reply to Pilate's false claim to power: "Unless it had been given from above." Jesus' death is not the victory of his enemies but follows the divine plan. His willing self-offering does not, however, exempt any of those involved in bringing about his death from sin. "If you release Him, you are not Caesar's friend." 'Friend of Caesar' is a honorific title, bestowed on persons in recognition of their special service to the emperor. These are persons of special influence. In order to compel Pilate to execute Jesus, the authorities have shifted away from their religious charge against Jesus to a political charge that He makes Himself King against Caesar, and they threaten to report Pilate as a 'traitor' to the emperor. The justice of this world is manifested: Pilate must hand over Jesus to the Jews to crucify to protect his political position and the Jews, ironically, portray themselves as loyal to the Roman Emperor (whose authority they really hate).

The Crucifixion of Jesus

Jesus is crucified as the exalted Son of God. When His heart was pierced with a lance He was dead and blood and water flowed from His heart but His mother's living heart was also pierced, as predicted by Simeon. Mary therefore assumed the motherhood of the new kingdom. Christ himself confirmed this when He entrusted mankind through John to His sorrowful mother. We note also that the death of Jesus is described as the handing over of the Spirit.

"What I Have Written"

By insisting that his inscription that Jesus was a king should stand as written, Pilate affirms the truth about Jesus. Pilate also emphasises the public and universal character of the inscription, since it could be read by all: Jews, Greeks and Romans.

Entrusting the Beloved Disciple and His mother to each other shows that Jesus' mission is completed but, significantly, there is a hint of a new Eve giving birth to her children.

"It is Finished"

His mission from the Father is now completed. Jesus 'hands over' His Spirit, a reminder that no one has 'taken' Jesus' life. He has given His life willingly.

Blood and water flows from the side of Christ. Water is the Spirit which the glorified Jesus will bestow on his followers. The blood (death) of Jesus is necessary for salvation.

The Spiritual Impact of Chapter 19 of St John's Gospel on Saint Faustina

Let us explore the spiritual impact on Saint Faustina and reflect on why our Lord wished the Saint (and us) to learn from the gospel passage.

Saint Faustina describes her feelings as follows: "During this reading, my soul was filled with deep repentance. I saw all the ingratitude of creatures toward their Creator and Lord; I asked God to protect me from spiritual blindness." (Diary 1766)

From the saint's interior vision, it is clear that we are all called to meditate on the immense power, majesty, glory and mercy of Our Lord and what He means to us in terms of our existence and our redemption. The saint's emotions point to the failure of mankind to reciprocate adequately God's generosity. This failure caused by spiritual blindness means mankind has failed to adequately meditate on Christ's identity and His redemptive mission on earth.

Through the gospel passage and Saint Faustina's interior vision, we are led to reflect on the spiritual immensity of the suffering servant of God, Our Lord Jesus Christ. He was the voice of the Father when the famous words of creation were uttered: "Let there be light"; "Let us make Man in our own image, in the likeness of ourselves, and let us be masters of the fish of the sea, the birds of heaven, the cattle, all the wild animals and all the creatures that creep along the ground." Christ, the Word, was the voice that spoke to Moses, the prophets and the holy people in the Old Testament. It was about Christ, then the suffering servant, that God confirmed as His Son during His baptism by John the Baptist; It was Christ who at Mount Tabor was confirmed by God the Father as His beloved Son and who elevated Him to the glorified body of our salvation. It was Christ, the Son of God, who, in obedience to His Father endured the sorrowful suffering to rescue the whole of mankind and human history from eternal bondage and damnation.

Scripture affirms that the Christ we see in St John's passage is God and all things in Heaven and on Earth, including humans and angels, were created in Him, through Him and for Him. The stability of humans, angels and all creation depends on Him. He is the source of life for all those who will be admitted into the new kingdom. All those who reject Him because their lives are unfit for the new kingdom of Heaven are described as rebels who then will follow the leader of the spiritual rebels into damnation.

On Rescuing Souls Through Sacrifice and Prayer

Christ to Saint Faustina: "My daughter, I want to instruct you on how you are to rescue souls through sacrifice and prayer. You will save more souls through prayer and suffering than will a missionary through his teachings and sermons alone. I want to see you as a sacrifice of living love, which only then carries weight before Me. You must be annihilated, destroyed, living as if you were dead in the most secret depths of your being. You must be destroyed in that secret depth where the human eye has never penetrated; then will I find in you a pleasing sacrifice, a holocaust full of sweetness and fragrance. And great will be your power for whomever you intercede. Outwardly, your sacrifice must look like this: silent, hidden, permeated with love, imbued with prayer. I demand, My daughter, that your sacrifice be pure and full of humility, that I may find pleasure in it. I will not spare My grace, that you may be able to fulfil what I demand of you.

"I will not instruct you on what your holocaust shall consist of, in every day life, so as to preserve you from illusions. You shall accept all sufferings with love. Do not be afflicted if your heart often experiences repugnance and dislike for sacrifice. All its power rests in the will, and so these contrary feelings, far from lowering the value of the sacrifice in My eyes, will enhance it. Know that your body and soul will often be in the midst of fire. Although you will not feel My presence on some occasions, I will always be with you. Do not fear; My grace will be with you." (Diary 1767)

Christ reveals to Saint Faustina the extraordinary efficacy of prayer and sacrifice in rescuing sinful souls; more efficacious than missionary work and sermons. However, to achieve the maximum benefit to souls in peril, certain conditions are necessary: interior mortifications provided that they are endured in a proper spiritual disposition. Christ assures us that, provided we direct our will, His grace will help us to triumph.

To have the will for sacrifice and prayer, we must always have the life and death of Christ as our model. His passion instructs us all the time. Christ's charity and love for sacrifice and prayer are displayed as follows: when He suffered, He did not threaten but prayed for those who judged Him unjustly. In the Garden of Gethsemane He prayed for the Father's will. Therefore during prayers and sacrifices for the rescue of sinful souls, we are uniting ourselves with the Passion of Christ, the perfect sacrifice that God accepts. By rebelling against sacrifices, we are diminishing the spiritual value of the sacrifice since we, the servants, cannot be greater than our master and saviour.

On Praying Especially for Souls That Offend Us or Frustrate Spiritual Progress

Christ is aware that there are Christians who believe they are acting for Him and yet frustrate faithful souls who are working for His purposes and plans of salvation. Just before the retreat, He had said the following to Saint Faustina about these self-appointed arbiters of God's designs:

"How can they sit on the promised throne of judgement to judge the world, when their guilt is greater than the guilt of the world? There is neither penance nor atonement. O heart, which received Me in the morning and at noon are all ablaze with hatred against Me, hatred of all sorts! O heart specially chosen by Me, were you chosen for this, to give Me more pain? The great sins of the world are superficial wounds on My heart, but the sins of a chosen soul pierce My heart through and through..." (Diary 1702)

Christ Calls for True Charity

Elsewhere in the Diary, Christ explains that even frustrations may be in accordance with His holy will.

Christ to Saint Faustina: **"To confirm your spirit, I speak through My representatives in accordance with what I demand of you, but know that this will not always be so. They will oppose you in many things, and through this My grace will be manifest in you, and it will be evident that this matter is**

My doing. But as for you, fear nothing; I am always with you. And know this, too, My daughter: all creatures whether they know it or not, and whether they want to or not, always fulfil My will." (Diary 586)

So as we undergo interior mortifications and prayer for the rescue of souls, in fulfilment of Divine will, we must constantly meditate on the spiritual benefits that attend the sacrifices. Let souls reflect on the observations of St Dorotheus: "But surely if a person were to examine himself carefully in the light of the fear of God he will never find that he is blameless. He will see that he has provided an occasion by some action or word or attitude. Even if such a one finds himself guiltless in all these ways at the present time, it is quite likely that at some other time he has vexed his brother by the very same deed or by some other."

St Dorotheus comments further on the behaviour of persons who reject interior mortifications. She believes that souls who react angrily to provocation already had traces of anger in them even before the provocation and they were only waiting to explode. The saint reasons that, if we have a pure heart, then because of that spiritual disposition, we shall be able to deal calmly with all temptations and trials. The saint counsels that as the soul advances in virtue it becomes stronger and better able to endure hardships that may come its way.

Suffering According to the Catechism and Traditions of the Church

The Catechism of the Catholic Church explains suffering as follows: "Suffering, a consequence of the original sin, acquires a new meaning; it becomes a participation in the saving work of Jesus." The Catechism goes on to explain that by His Passion and death on the cross, Christ has given a new meaning to suffering because it unites us to Christ's redemptive Passion. Saint Paul teaches that we are made perfect through our afflictions because in suffering in the flesh, we are completing what is lacking in Christ's afflictions for the sake of his mystical Body.

Saint Augustine says this on suffering: "You are suffering as much as was to be contributed from your sufferings to the whole suffering of Christ, who suffered as our head, and suffers in his members, that is, in ourselves.

"To this common republic of ours, so to say, each of us according to his measure pays what he owes and we contribute as it were a quota of suffering according to the powers that we possess. The storehouse of all men's sufferings will not have been filled until the world has come to an end."

In effect, what St Augustine is telling us is that when Christ assumed the nature of man to suffer pains and humiliation to redeem us, he bore a sacrifice, the debt of which all conceivable human sacrifices can never pay. If our sacrifices and penances are to be accepted by God, then they must first be united to the sacrifices of Christ. The Divine Mercy is then able to flow freely to bestow graces to enable us to overcome all challenges.

Suffering also explains how humanity is able to share the Trinitarian life. It is from the most perfect love that exists between God the Father and God the Son, that the Holy Spirit proceeds and becomes the source of our life. When Christ became man, he repeated the same love to the Father through obedience and suffering. Through this same process, we receive the Holy Spirit because Christ made the sacrifice as the representative of all mankind. It is therefore through the sacrifice of the cross, that we receive the gift of life of the Holy Spirit.

The Third Day of the Retreat

The Eucharist: truest revelation of God's merciful love

Christ to Saint Faustina: "**Now you shall consider My love in the Blessed Sacrament. Here, I am entirely yours, soul, body and divinity, as your bridegroom. You know what love demands; only thing only, reciprocity.**" (Diary 1770)

If we have the faith to contemplate the majesty, splendour and glory of Christ truly present in the Blessed Sacrament, there is infused into us God's love as we contemplate the weakness and humiliation Christ took on Himself as Man. We are transformed into the life of Christ's glorified Body and inwardly assured of the restoration of the perfect nature God gave us at the dawn of creation.

From sinful nature, we have been ushered into a new kingdom of God through the flesh of the Eucharist.

The Eucharist is the greatest, visible source of hope, joy and glory. It is the greatest source of consolation because Christ, as Lord and God, came to join our humiliation and misery, through his death and resurrection. We behold in the Blessed Sacrament, the total show of God's merciful love for mankind.

If we have faith, the contemplation before the Blessed Sacrament and receiving of Eucharist become our greatest joy and our greatest experience of Godhead. We experience the fulness of this love which interiorly raises us to the supernatural bond with God, generating an interchange of ideas, exposing our trials and tribulation before Him and He enkindles in us the greatest consolations and spiritual gifts to enable us to overcome the world, the Devil and the flesh.

Contemplating the Blessed Sacrament or worthily receiving the Blessed Sacrament is the truest way to sanctification and responding to God's love.

Christ to Saint Faustina: **"Today, for your spiritual reading, you will take the Gospel of St John, Chapter twenty-one. Let it feed your heart more than your mind."** (Diary 1773)

Chapter 21 of St John's Gospel

"Later on, Jesus revealed Himself again to the disciples. It was by the Sea of Tiberias, and it happened like this: Simon Peter, Thomas called the Twin, Nathanael from Cana in Galilee, the sons of Zebedee and two more of his disciples were together. Simon Peter said, 'I'm going fishing.' They replied, 'We'll come with you.' They went out and got into the boat but caught nothing that night.

"When it was already light, there stood Jesus on the shore, though the disciples did not realise that it was Jesus. Jesus called out, 'Haven't you caught anything, friends?' And when they answered, 'No,' He said, 'Throw the net out to starboard and you'll find something.'

So they threw the net out and could not haul it in because of the quantity of fish. The disciple whom Jesus loved said to Peter, 'It is the Lord.' At these words, 'It is the Lord,' Simon Peter tied his outer garment round him and jumped into the water. The other disciples came on in the boat, towing the net with the fish; they were only about a hundred yards from land.

"As soon as they came ashore they saw that there was some bread there and a charcoal fire with fish cooking on it. Jesus said, 'Bring some of the fish you have just caught.' Simon Peter went aboard and dragged the net ashore, full of big fish, one hundred and fifty-three of them; and in spite of there being so many the net was not broken. Jesus said to them, 'Come and have breakfast.' None of the disciples was bold enough to ask, 'Who are You?' They knew quite well it was the Lord. Jesus then stepped forward, took the bread and gave it to them, and the same with the fish. This was the third time that Jesus revealed Himself to the disciples after rising from the dead.

"When they had eaten, Jesus said to Simon Peter, 'Simon, son of John, do you love me more than these others do?' He answered, 'Yes, Lord, You know I love you.' Jesus said to him, 'Feed my lambs.' A second time He said to him, 'Simon, son of John, do you love Me?' He replied, 'Yes, Lord, You know I love You.' Jesus said to him, 'Look after my sheep.' Then He said to him a third time, 'Simon, son of John, do you love Me?'. Peter was hurt that He asked him a third time, 'Do you love Me?' and said, 'Lord, You know everything; You know I love You.' Jesus said to him,

> Feed my sheep.
> In all truth I tell you,
> when you were young,
> you put on your own belt,
> and walked where you liked;
> but when you grow old,
> you will stretch out your hands,
> and somebody else

will put a belt round you
and take you
where you would rather not go.

In these words He indicated the kind of death which Peter would give glory to God. After this He said, 'Follow Me.'

Peter turned and saw the disciple whom Jesus loved following them – the one who had leant back close to His chest at the supper and had said to Him, 'Lord, who is it that will betray You?'' Seeing Him, Peter said to Jesus, 'What about him, Lord?'" Jesus answered, 'If I want him to stay behind till I come, what does it matter to you? You are to follow Me.' The rumour then went out among the brothers that this disciple would not die. Yet Jesus had not said to Peter, 'He will not die,' but, 'If I want him to stay behind till I come, what does it matter to you?'

This disciple is the one who vouches for these things and has written them down, and we know that his testimony is true.

There was much else that Jesus did; if it were written down in detail, I do not suppose the world itself would hold all the books that would be written.

Reflections: the miraculous catch of fish

The account of the miraculous catch of fish confirms the necessity of Christ in all works of redemption. Jesus' command to the disciples to cast their nets, resulting in the great catch of fish indicates that Christ will continue to be with the disciples even after His resurrection.

The resurrection appearance story also confirms the tradition in which Jesus' presence is recognised in the Eucharistic meal. The presence of Peter in the story is significant in reminding us of how Christ patiently prepares weak souls to perfection. In the story Peter is offered the opportunity to make a triple affirmation of love. From the words of Jesus, it is confirmed that loving Jesus means keeping His commands in the new profession of love. Peter as the new shepherd of Jesus ' flock is commanded to express this love by feeding and shepherding the new members of Jesus' flock. Jesus then predicts a martyr's death for Peter : "Somebody else will put a belt around you and take you where you would rather not go."

Conference on Mercy

Christ to Saint Faustina: "**My daughter, know that My Heart is mercy itself.** From this sea of mercy, graces flow out upon the whole world. No soul that has approached Me has ever gone away unconsoled. All misery gets buried in the depths of My mercy, and every saving and sanctifying grace flows from this fountain. My daughter, I desire that your heart be an abiding place of My mercy. I desire that this mercy flow out upon the whole world through your heart. Let no one who approaches you go away without that trust in My mercy which I so ardently desire for souls.

"**Pray as much as you can for the dying.** By your entreaties, obtain for them trust in My mercy, because they have most need of trust, and have it the least. Be assured that the grace of eternal salvation for certain souls in their final moment depends on your prayer. You know the whole abyss of My mercy, so draw upon it for yourself and especially for poor sinners. Sooner would Heaven and Earth turn into nothingness than would My mercy not embrace a trusting soul."(Diary 1777)

Let us reflect on the following themes raised by Our Lord Jesus Christ.
1 His Sacred Heart as the source of Divine Mercy;
2 Souls in misery and needing consolation and /or salvation;
3 The role of faithful souls

Sacred Heart: source of mercy

Scripture: The revelation of the truth that God is love is manifested to humans in the Heart of Jesus. Christ gives the hint of this symbol and reality in St John's gospel when foretelling His approaching death: He cried out: "Let anyone who is thirsty come to Me! Let anyone who believes in Me come and drink! As scripture says, 'From

His heart shall flow streams of living water.'" (John 7:37-38).

St John explains: "He was speaking of the Spirit which those who believed in Him were to receive; for there was no Spirit as yet because Jesus had not yet been glorified." (John 7:39)

The gospel writer then dramatically gives the account of the pierced side of Jesus, with blood and water flowing from His side: "It was the Day of Preparation" (John 19:33-37). St John is careful to emphasise the truth of the story, apparently because of its importance for our salvation. From Christ's own reference to water streaming from the Heart, He is telling us that the water and blood from the pierced side were flowing from His Heart.

Christ confirms the symbol and reality of His merciful Heart in the Diary: "My Heart overflows with great mercy for souls, and especially for poor sinners. If only they could understand that I am the best of Fathers to them and that it is for them that Blood and Water flowed from My Heart as from a fount overflowing with mercy. For them I dwell in the tabernacle as King of Mercy. I desire to bestow My graces upon souls, but they do not want to accept them." (Diary 367)

We may further reflect on the union of the Heart of Jesus and the Heart of Mary, remembering that Mary conceived Christ according to the flesh and therefore Christ's flesh was formed from Mary's flesh. The Heart of Jesus pierced for our sins and for our salvation comes from the flesh of Mary and it is not surprising that Simeon, foreseeing in Spirit Christ's agony and passion, prophesied to Mary in the Temple, that her heart, alongside that of her son, would be pierced with a sword. Mary's heart thus, in God's plan of salvation, becomes united in suffering with that of her divine Son. She becomes the perfect participant humanly imaginable in God's redemptive love.

The Heart of Jesus now continues to perform salvific work in His glorified Body. Having been glorified by His Father because His sacrifice has pleased His Father, Christ has been invested with sovereign authority and as judge, fully entrusted with the destiny of all creatures. However His merciful Heart is within His glorified

Body and He is also our Advocate before the Father. Of this role St Mechtilde was privileged to see in a vision: "All the graces which God increasingly pours forth on man, according to the capacity of each, come from the plenitude of the Divine Heart." Until the fulness of time, then, Christ's merciful Heart sends the gifts of the Spirit upon humanity to enable us to obtain salvation.

Summary of the Mysteries of the Heart of Jesus

1   God is love, a love that is so immense that we cannot conceive it by our senses. It is spiritual and its extent is beyond our understanding.

2   God sent His Son, our Lord Jesus Christ, so that by His life and death we may have some understanding of His love.

3   In a mysterious way, He uses the Heart of Christ as a symbol and reality of this love.

4   When we see the Heart, pierced by the lance, for our sake, it evokes feelings of shock and remorse.

5   When St Margaret Mary became aware of Christ's sufferings as manifested through his pierced Heart, she became fully devoted to the merciful Heart. She said that guided by the Spirit, she could do only five things: 1) to love her divine Saviour Jesus Christ with an extreme love 2) to obey perfectly after the example of Jesus Christ 3) to wish for suffering ceaselessly for the love of Jesus Christ 4) to wish to suffer in silence with an insatiable hunger to receive Holy Communion, to adore the most Blessed Sacrament, to be humiliated, to live poor, unknown and despised by all, and finally to live overwhelmed with all kinds of infirmities and miseries.

The saint was shocked by the heavenly power of Christ contrasted with his earthly sufferings and afflictions. Seeing and reflecting on the merciful Heart of Jesus should therefore induce in us a realisation of our sinfulness and ingratitude and the strongest desire to make reparations and sacrifices for our salvation and for other sinful souls.

Souls in Misery

Saint Faustina keeps referring in the Diary to Christ's call to souls in their misery. From these accounts, it becomes clear that all souls, whatever the state of their spiritual life are subject to despair and misery.

One category of the miserable souls Christ laments about are those who do not care about their eternal destiny, whence they came and where they are going or even the meaning of life. Many souls are in this state even though, according to St Augustine, God has created us for Himself and souls are restless until they turn to Him. The Creator of all things creates occasions and circumstances for all sincere souls to find Him.

In his introduction to the Vatican II document, *Lumen Gentium,* Cardinal Paul Poupard refers to those Christians and others who feel the need for spirituality and yet rebel against what he refers to as the "ordered, structured, timeless and revealed faith of the creed", preferring rather a "self-centred spirituality". The cardinal goes on to explain as follows: "God is often ignored and common indifference, errant belief and selfishness seem in our day to lead people to say 'yes' to some sort of religious feeling, but no to God and no to the Church." The cardinal emphasizes as follows: "It is a Church that orientates our belief in God and that we profess One, Holy, Catholic and Apostolic Church."

In Saint Faustina's diary, Christ mentions "lukewarm" souls as the ones who caused Him most suffering during His agony. These are souls who deliberately fail to overcome their weaknesses and are therefore unable to respond to the graces flowing to them from Christ's sacrifice. They do not therefore have the spiritual dispositions necessary for them to accomplish God's purpose. These souls are occupied with many external distractions or occupations aimed only at promoting their material well being, to the extent that their spiritual life is pushed to the extreme margins. Religious life for these souls becomes a casual commitment. These souls are in a state where they cannot hear the voice of God calling upon them to turn to Him. These souls do not reflect fully on the price that Christ paid for our redemption.

In an episode in the Diary, Christ appeared to Saint Faustina and asked her to help a dying person: **"My daughter, help me to save souls. You will go to a dying sinner, and you will continue to recite the Chaplet, and in this way you will obtain for him trust in My mercy, for he is already in despair."** (Diary 1797) Saint Faustina recounts her intervention as follows: "Suddenly, I found myself in a strange cottage where an elderly man was dying amidst great torments. All about the bed was a multitude of demons and the family, who were crying. When I began to pray, the spirits of darkness fled, with hissing and threats directed at me. The soul became calm and filled with trust, rested in the Lord." (Diary 1798) Christ, by this example, reminds faithful souls of the gospel message of salvation and our obligation to assist souls through our prayers and sacrifices.

Christ is also mindful of His mercy towards faithful souls who have responded to His merciful love and yet experience feelings of remorse because of their inner feelings that they have not done enough to merit God's mercy and love. On her death bed, St Bernadette complained that she had not done enough, when she contemplated what gifts she had received. Likewise St Catherine of Siena experienced great misery, because she saw her unworthiness before God, to the extent that she felt that she was the cause of all the evil in the world and prayed as follows: "O Eternal Father, I accuse myself before You, in order that You may punish me for my sins in this finite life, and, inasmuch as my sins are the cause of the sufferings which my neighbour must endure, I implore You, in Your kindness, to punish them in my person."

Even the saints experienced spiritual miseries. They received many sacramental gifts and yet they felt spiritually inadequate. The merciful Heart of Jesus calls on all faithful souls to learn from the experience of the saints. All souls are called upon by His heart to trust Him because the graces flowing from His merciful Heart are effective in restoring them to spiritual perfection and salvation. Indeed He anticipates our actions with the necessary graces.

There is yet another dimension to this state of misery. In St Catherine's encounter with God, it was explained that these feelings of misery may be temptations by the Devil but the saint was assured that God is faithful to those who put their trust in Him: God revealed to St Catherine as follows. "And no one should fear any battle or temptation of the Devil that may come to him, because I have made My creatures strong, and have given them strength of will, fortified in the Blood of my Son, which will neither Devil nor creature can move, because it is yours, given by Me. You therefore, with free arbitration, can hold it or leave it, according as you please. It is an arm, which, if you place it in the hands of the Devil, straightaway becomes a knife, with which he strikes you and slays you. But if man do not give this knife of his will into the hands of the Devil, that is, if he do not consent to his temptations and molestations, he will never be injured by the guilt of sin in any temptation, but will even be fortified by it, when the eye of his intellect is opened to see My love which allowed him to be tempted, so as to arrive at virtue, by being proved. For one does not arrive at virtue except through knowledge of self, and knowledge of Me, which knowledge is more perfectly acquired in the time of temptation, because then Man knows himself to be nothing, being unable to lift off himself the pains and vexations which he would flee; and he knows Me in his will, which is fortified by My goodness, so that it does not yield to these thoughts. And he has seen that My love permits these temptations, for the Devil is weak, and by himself can do nothing unless I allow him." (The Dialogue of St Catherine of Siena)

In her diary, St Faustina recounts an interior voice that made her feel as follows: "You see, God is so holy, and you are sinful. Do not approach Him, and go to Confession every day." (Diary 1802)

The saint was thrown into a state of misery "And indeed, whatever I thought of seemed to me to be a sin" (Diary 1802). She then recounts her experience in the confessional: "However, in the confessional, God allowed me to accuse myself of only two imperfections, despite my efforts to make a confession according to what I had prepared. When I left the confessional, the Lord told me, 'My daughter, all those sins you intended to confess are not sins in My eyes; that is why I took away your ability to tell them.' I understood that Satan, wanting to disturb my peace, has been giving me exaggerated thoughts." (Diary 1802)

From Christ's merciful heart, therefore, graces flow upon all souls in misery, restoring those who have the will and trust to receive them. The ultimate jotting in Saint Faustina's diary should be, to all mankind, a message of great and kind hope. "Today, the Majesty of God is surrounding me. There is no way that I can help myself to prepare better. I am thoroughly enwrapped in God. My soul is being inflamed by His love. I only know that I love and am loved. That is enough for me. I am trying my best to be faithful throughout the day to the Holy Spirit and to fulfil His demands. I am trying my best for interior silence to be able to hear His voice." (Diary 1828)

Indeed, God our Creator and true end constantly speaks to all His children, inviting them to come nearer and nearer to obtain peace and purity of spirit and soul.

CHAPTER 2

Divine Mercy Devotions

During repeated revelations to Saint Faustina, our Lord requested five forms of devotion to the Divine Mercy. These are:

1   The Feast of Mercy
2   The Novena to the Divine Mercy
3   Image of the Divine Mercy
4   The Chaplet of Divine Mercy
5   The Hour of Mercy

Introduction to the devotions

Devotions are exterior actions which really and deeply express the interior disposition of the person based on the love of God who saves him through the merciful actions of His Son. The devotions are intended to perfect and strengthen our faith and inspire in us God's strength and consolation to overcome all the spiritual and earthly challenges to our redemption. By performing these devotions, we come to deepen our understanding of the spiritual gifts flowing to mankind from Christ's sacrifice of redemption. Finally, we are enabled to inspire fervour not only in ourselves but in our fellow humans and then contribute to their redemption. By these devotions, God in his mercy makes actual in ourselves, through the Holy Spirit, the treasures acquired for mankind through Christ's sacrificial life.

In Saint Faustina's diary, Christ confirms through the saint that the devotions are truly meant for our salvation and requests her to communicate His authority as follows: **"My daughter, be at peace;**

do as I tell you. Your thoughts are united to My thoughts, so write whatever comes to your mind. You are the secretary of My mercy. I have chosen you for that office in this life and the next life. That is how I want it to be in spite of all the opposition they will give you. Know that My choice will not change." (Diary 1605)

Through Saint Faustina, Christ comes back to mankind to restore us out of our misery and despair. He reminds us that God has been faithful to mankind from the fall of our first parents and that he continues to bestow gifts of grace through Christ's eternal sacrifice.

The Feast of Mercy

The feast links the paschal mystery of redemption and the mystery of Divine Mercy. Christ requests a novena which begins on Good Friday and is celebrated on the Sunday after Easter.

In her diary, Saint Faustina wrote that Jesus told her: "On each day of the novena you will bring to My Heart a different group of souls and you will immerse them in this ocean of My mercy … On each day you will beg My Father, on the strength of My bitter Passion, for graces for these souls." (Diary 1209)

Novena to the Divine Mercy

Christ to Saint Faustina: **"I desire that during these nine days you bring souls to the fountain of My mercy, that they may draw therefrom strength and refreshment and whatever grace they need in the hardships of life, and especially, at the hour of death. On each day you will bring to My Heart a different group of souls, and you will immerse them in this ocean of My mercy, and I will bring all these souls into the house of My Father. You will do this in this life and in the next. I will deny nothing to any soul whom you will bring to the fount of My mercy. On each day you will beg My Father, on the strength of My bitter Passion, for graces for these souls."** (Diary 1209)

First Day

Christ to Saint Faustina: "Today bring to Me all mankind, especially all sinners, and immerse them in the ocean of My mercy. In this way you will console Me in the bitter grief into which the loss of souls plunges Me."

Most Merciful Jesus, whose very nature it is to have compassion on us and to forgive us, do not look upon our sins but upon our trust which we place in Your infinite goodness. Receive us all into the abode of Your Most Compassionate Heart, and never let us escape from It. We beg this of You by Your love which unites You to the Father and the Holy Spirit.

Eternal Father, turn Your merciful gaze upon all mankind and especially upon poor sinners, all enfolded in the Most Compassionate Heart of Jesus. For the sake of His sorrowful Passion show us Your mercy, that we may praise the omnipotence of Your mercy forever and ever. Amen.

(Then pray the Chaplet to the Divine Mercy)

Second Day

Christ to Saint Faustina: "Today bring to Me the souls of priests and religious, and immerse them in My unfathomable mercy. It was they who gave Me strength to endure My bitter Passion. Through them, as through channels, My mercy flows upon mankind."

Most Merciful Jesus, from whom comes all that is good, increase Your grace in us, that we may perform worthy works of mercy, consecrated to Your service, that they may perform worthy works of mercy; and that all who see them may glorify the Father of Mercy who is in heaven.

Eternal Father, turn Your merciful gaze upon the company of chosen ones in your vineyard – upon the souls of priests and religious; and endow them with the strength of Your blessing. For the love of the Heart of Your Son in which they are enfolded, impart to them Your power and light, that they may be able to guide others in the way of salvation and with one voice sing praise to Your boundless mercy for ages without end. Amen.

(Then pray the Chaplet to the Divine Mercy)

Third Day
Christ to Saint Faustina: **"Today bring to Me all devout and faithful souls, immerse them in the ocean of My mercy. These souls brought me consolation on the Way of the Cross. They were that drop of consolation in the midst of an ocean of bitterness."**

Most Merciful Jesus, from the treasury of Your mercy, You impart Your graces in great abundance to each and all. Receive us into the abode of Your Most Compassionate Heart and never let us escape from It. We beg this grace of You by that most wondrous love for the heavenly Father with which Your Heart burns so fiercely.

Eternal Father, turn Your merciful gaze upon faithful souls, as upon the inheritance of Your Son. For the sake of His sorrowful Passion, grant them Your blessing and surround them with Your constant protection. Thus may they never fail in love or lose the treasure of the holy faith, but rather, with all the hosts of angels and saints, may they glorify Your boundless mercy for endless ages. Amen.

(Then pray the Chaplet to the Divine Mercy)

Fourth Day
Christ to Saint Faustina: **"Today bring to Me the pagans and those who do not yet know me. I was thinking also of them during My bitter Passion, and their future zeal comforted My Heart. Immerse them in the ocean of My mercy."**

Most compassionate Jesus, You are the Light of the whole world. Receive into the abode of Your Most Compassionate Heart the souls of pagans who as yet do not know You. Let the rays of Your grace enlighten them that they, too, together with us, may extol Your wonderful mercy; and do not let them escape from the abode which is Your Most Compassionate Heart.

Eternal Father, turn Your merciful gaze upon the souls of pagans and who as yet do not know You, but who are enclosed in the Most Compassionate Heart of Jesus. Draw them to the light of the Gospel. These souls do not know what great happiness it is to love You. Grant that they, too, may extol the generosity of Your mercy for endless ages. Amen.

(Then pray the Chaplet to the Divine Mercy)

Fifth Day
Christ to Saint Faustina: **"Today bring to Me the souls of heretics and schismatics and immerse them in the ocean of My mercy. During My bitter passion they tore at My Body and Heart, that is, My Church. As they return to unity with the Church, My wounds heal and in this way they alleviate My Passion."**

Most Merciful Jesus, Goodness Itself, You do not refuse light to those who seek it of You. Receive into the abode of Your Most Compassionate Heart the souls of heretics and schismatics. Draw them by Your light into the unity of the Church, and do not let them escape from the abode of Your Most Compassionate Heart; but bring it about that they, too, come to glorify the generosity of Your mercy.

Eternal Father, turn Your merciful gaze upon the souls of heretics and schismatics, who have squandered Your blessings and misused Your graces by obstinately persisting in their errors. Do not look upon their errors, but upon the love of Your own Son and upon His bitter Passion, which He underwent for their sake, since they, too, are enclosed in His Most Compassionate Heart of Jesus. Bring it about that they also may glorify Your great mercy for endless ages. Amen.

(Then pray the Chaplet to the Divine Mercy)

Sixth Day

Christ to Saint Faustina: **"Today bring to Me the meek and humble souls and the souls of little children, and immerse them in My mercy. These souls most closely resemble My Heart. They strengthened Me during My bitter agony. I saw them as earthly angels, who will keep vigil at My altars. I pour out upon them whole torrents of grace. Only the humble soul is capable of receiving My grace. I favour humble souls with My confidence."**

Most Merciful Jesus, You yourself have said, "Learn from Me for I am meek and humble of heart." Receive into the abode of Your Most Compassionate Heart all meek and humble souls and the souls of little children. These souls send all Heaven into ecstasy and they are the heavenly Father's favourites. They are a sweet-smelling bouquet before the throne of God; God Himself takes delight in their fragrance. These souls have a permanent abode in Your Most Compassionate Heart, O Jesus, and they unceasingly sing out a hymn of love and mercy.

Eternal Father, turn Your merciful gaze upon meek and humble souls, and upon little children who are enfolded in the abode which is the Most Compassionate Heart of Jesus. These souls bear the closest resemblance to Your Son. Their fragrance rises from the Earth and reaches Your very throne. Father of mercy and of all goodness, I beg You by the love You bear these souls and by the delight You take in them: Bless the whole world, that all souls together may sing out the praises of Your mercy for endless ages. Amen.

(Then pray the Chaplet to the Divine Mercy)

Seventh Day

Christ to Saint Faustina: "Today bring to Me the souls who especially venerate and glorify My mercy, and immerse them in My mercy. These souls sorrowed most over my Passion and entered most deeply into My spirit. They are living images of My Compassionate Heart. These souls will shine with a special brightness in the next life. Not one of them will go into the fire of hell. I shall particularly defend each one of them at the hour of death."

Most Merciful Jesus, whose Heart is Love Itself, receive into the abode of Your Most Compassionate Heart the souls of those who particularly extol and venerate the greatness of Your mercy. These souls are mighty with the very power of God Himself. In the midst of all afflictions and adversities they go forward, confident of Your mercy. These souls are united to Jesus and carry all mankind on their shoulders. These souls will not be judged severely, but Your mercy will embrace them as they depart from this life.

Eternal Father, turn Your merciful gaze upon the souls who glorify and venerate Your greatest attribute, that of Your fathomless mercy, and who are enclosed in the Most Compassionate Heart of Jesus. These souls are a living Gospel; their hands are full of deeds of mercy, and their spirits, overflowing with joy, sing a canticle of mercy to You, O Most High! I beg You O God: Show them Your mercy according to the hope and trust they have placed in You. Let there be accomplished in them the promise of Jesus, who said to them, **'I Myself will defend as My own glory, during their lifetime, and especially at the hour of their death, those souls who will venerate My fathomless mercy.'** Amen.

(Then pray the Chaplet to the Divine Mercy)

Eighth Day

Christ to Saint Faustina: **"Today bring to Me the souls who are in the prison of purgatory, and immerse them in the** abyss of My mercy. Let the torrents of My Blood cool down their scorching flames. All these souls are greatly loved by Me. They are making retribution to My justice. It is in your power to bring them relief. Draw all the indulgences from the treasury of My Church and offer them on their behalf. Oh, if you only knew the torments they suffer, you would continually offer for them the alms of the spirit and pay off their debt to My justice."

Most Merciful Jesus, You Yourself have said that You desire mercy; so I bring into the abode of Your Most Compassionate Heart the souls in purgatory, souls who are very dear to You, and yet, who must make retribution to Your justice. May the streams of blood and water which gushed forth from Your Heart put out the flames of purifying fire, that in the place, too, the power of Your mercy may be praised.

Eternal Father, turn Your merciful gaze upon the souls suffering in purgatory, who are enfolded in the Most Compassionate Heart of Jesus. I beg You, by the sorrowful Passion of Jesus Your Son, and by all the bitterness with which His most sacred Soul was flooded, manifest Your mercy to the souls who are under Your just scrutiny. Look upon them in no other way but only through the Wounds of Jesus, Your dearly beloved Son; for we firmly believe that there is no limit to Your goodness and compassion. Amen.

(Then pray the Chaplet to the Divine Mercy)

Ninth Day
Christ to Saint Faustina: "Today bring to Me souls who have become lukewarm, and immerse them in the abyss of My mercy. These souls wound My Heart most painfully. My soul suffered the most dreadful loathing in the Garden of Olives because of lukewarm souls. They were the reason I cried out: "Father, take this cup away from Me, if it be Your will." For them, the last hope of salvation is flee to My mercy."

Most compassionate Jesus, You are Compassion Itself. I bring lukewarm souls into the abode of Your Most Compassionate Heart. In this fire of Your pure love, let these tepid souls, who, like corpses, filled You with such deep loathing, be once again set aflame. O Most Compassionate Jesus, exercise the omnipotence of Your mercy and draw them into the very ardour of Your love, and bestow upon them the gift of holy love, for nothing is beyond Your power.

Eternal Father, turn Your merciful gaze upon lukewarm souls who are nonetheless enfolded in the Most Compassionate Heart of Jesus. Father of Mercy, I beg You by the bitter Passion of Your Son and by His three hour agony on the cross: Let them, too, glorify the abyss of Your mercy. Amen.
(Then pray the Chaplet to the Divine Mercy)

Concerning the Feast of Mercy Jesus said: **"Whoever approaches the Fount of Life on this day will be granted complete forgiveness of sins and punishment."** (Diary 300)

"I want the image solemnly blessed on the first Sunday after Easter, and I want it to be venerated publicly so that every soul may know about it."(Diary 341)

"This Feast emerged from the very depths of My mercy, and it is confirmed in the vast depths of my tender mercies." (Diary 420)

Saint Faustina later revealed: "On one occasion, I heard these words: **'My daughter, tell the whole world about My inconceivable mercy. I desire that the Feast of Mercy be a refuge and shelter for all souls, and especially for poor sinners. On that day the very depths of My tender mercy are open. I pour out a whole ocean of graces upon those souls who approach the fount of Mercy. The soul that will go to Confession and receive Holy Communion shall obtain complete forgiveness of sins and** punishment. On that day all the divine floodgates through which grace flow are opened. Let no soul fear to draw near to Me, even though its sins be as scarlet. My mercy is so great that no mind, be it of man or of angel, will able to fathom it throughout all eternity. Everything that exists has come forth from the very depths of My most tender mercy. Every soul in its relation to Me will contemplate My love and mercy throughout eternity. The Feast of Mercy emerged from My very depths of tenderness. It is My desire that it be solemnly celebrated on the first Sunday after Easter. Mankind will not have peace until it turns to the Fount of My Mercy.'" (Diary 699)

"I demand from you deeds of mercy, which are to arise out of love for Me. You are to show mercy to your neighbours always and everywhere. You must not shrink from this or try to excuse or absolve yourself from it." (Diary 742)

"I want to grant complete pardon to the souls that will go to Confession and receive Holy Communion on the Feast of My mercy." (Diary 1109)

In summary, we must remember that Christ makes extraordinary promises for those who fulfil the conditions for the worthy celebration of the feast. He promises a complete remission of their sins and punishment. This means that, provided they have trust in God's goodness, show active love towards their neighbour and die in a state of sanctifying grace (confession and worthy reception of Communion), they will go straight to heaven without going through the purgative fire of purgatory.

The Image of the Divine Mercy

On 22nd February 1931, Jesus appeared to Saint Faustina with two rays of light radiating from His heart (a pale ray and a red ray). Jesus said: "Paint an image according to the pattern you see, with the signature: Jesus I trust in You. I desire that this image be venerated, first in your chapel and throughout the world." (Diary 47)

"I promise that the soul that will venerate this image will not perish. I also promise victory over its enemies already here on Earth, especially at the hour of death. I myself will defend it as My own glory." (Diary 48)

"I am offering people a vessel with which they are to keep coming for graces to the fountain of mercy. That vessel is this image with the signature: Jesus, I trust in You." (Diary 327)

"The two rays denote Blood and Water. The pale ray stands for the Water which makes souls righteous. The red ray stands for the Blood which is the life of souls. These two rays issued forth from the very depths of My tender mercy when My agonized Heart was opened by a lance on the Cross. These rays shield souls from the wrath of My Father. Happy is the one who dwells in their shelter, for the just hand of God shall not lay hold of him." (Diary 299)

"Not in the beauty of the colour, nor of the brush lies the greatness of this image, but in My grace." (Diary 313)

"By means of this image I shall grant many graces to souls. It is to be a reminder of the demands of My mercy, because even the strongest faith is of no avail without works." (Diary 742)

When Christ calls upon us to venerate the Image of the Divine Mercy, he is not asking us to venerate the painting itself but rather He wants us to be led to the mysteries to which the image leads us or to what it represents. The image is a vessel that reminds us of God's mercy. This image is revealing to us a fountain of graces flowing from the pierced Heart of Christ on the Cross. The water represents baptism, the gift of the Spirit which cleanses us of all our sins and the blood represents the Eucharist, Christ's gift of Himself to the Father to expiate our sins on the cross. So, the image of the pierced side of Christ pouring out blood and water reminds us that the Cross is the price of mercy. The image should help us to remember the terrible price paid to redeem us. Looking at the image, we should be distressed with St Teresa of Avila who in contemplation of God saw the extent of human ingratitude and put it as follows: "What has become of Christians now? Must those who owe you most always be those who distress you?" If we are able to look at the image with faith and trust, the Spirit will interiorly reveal the secrets of the water and blood and make us aware of our own sins and the mercy of God.

Christ promises to those who look at the image with eyes of faith eternal salvation and progress in Christian perfection. He promises the grace of a happy death and all other graces which people will ask of him with trust.

The Chaplet of Divine Mercy

In reciting the Chaplet, we are offering to God the Body, Blood, Soul and Divinity of our Lord Jesus Christ. We are affirming our belief that all our good actions can only proceed from the obedience and sacrifices of Christ which have been accepted by His Father. The Holy Spirit therefore draws from the treasures of Christ's sacrifices the gifts that enable us to have great merits before God, to become co-heirs with Christ and worthy of eternal life. So it is the glorified Body of Christ that we behold during the recitation of the Chaplet. But we are also reminded that it was through His Blood of sacrifice that showed the Father's love for His Son and how pleased He was with His obedience and sacrifice. The Chaplet is therefore a prayer of atonement which reconciles us to God and unites us to the sacrifice of Christ. It is a prayer that was dictated by Christ himself to Saint Faustina. When reciting the prayer, we are called upon to trust in God's mercy, to show humility and believe in the efficacy of Christ's redemptive act.

Christ promised Saint Faustina that all those who pray the Chaplet will receive the grace of conversion and have a peaceful death. He also promised that if the Chaplet is recited at the side of a dying person, he will have a peaceful death.

The Chaplet

1   Begin with the Sign of the Cross, 1 Our Father, 1 Hail Mary and The Apostles' Creed.
2   Then on the Our Father Beads say the following: Eternal Father, I offer You the Body and Blood, Soul and Divinity of Your dearly beloved Son, Our Lord Jesus Christ, in atonement for our sins and those of the whole world.
3   On the ten Hail Mary Beads say the following: For the sake of His sorrowful Passion, have mercy on us and on the whole world.
   (Repeat step two and three for all five decades)
4   Conclude with (three times): Holy God, Holy Mighty One, Holy Immortal One, have mercy on us and on the whole world.

The Hour of Mercy

Jesus asked Saint Faustina and through Saint Faustina, asked us, to celebrate this hour of great mercy, promising great graces to those who do this for themselves and on behalf of other people.

"At three o'clock, implore My mercy, especially for sinners; and, if only for a brief moment, immerse yourself in My Passion, particularly in My abandonment at the moment of agony. This is the hour of great mercy for the whole world... in this hour I will refuse nothing to the soul that makes a request of Me in virtue of My Passion."(*Diary* 1320).

"As often as you hear the clock strike the third hour immerse yourself completely in My mercy, adoring and glorifying it, invoke its omnipotence for the whole world, and particularly for poor sinners, for at that moment mercy was opened wide for every soul. In this hour you can obtain everything for yourself and for others for the asking; it was the hour of grace for the whole world – mercy triumphed over justice."

"Try your best to make the Stations of the Cross in this hour, provided that your duties permit it; and if you are not able to make the Stations of the Cross, then at least step into the chapel for a moment and adore, in the most Blessed Sacrament, My Heart, which is full of mercy: and should you be unable to step into chapel, immerse yourself in prayer there where you happen to be, if only for a very brief instant." (Diary 1572)

3 O'clock Prayers

You expired, Jesus, but the source of life gushed forth for souls and the ocean of mercy opened up for the whole world. O Fount of Life, unfathomable Divine Mercy, envelop the whole world and empty Yourself out upon us.

O blood and water, which gushed forth from the Heart of Jesus as a fount of mercy for us, I trust in You.

St Faustina's Way of the Cross : Opening Prayer

Merciful Lord, my Master, I want to follow You faithfully. I want to imitate You in my life in an ever more perfect way. That is why I ask that by meditating on Your Passion, You would grant me the grace of a deeper understanding of the mysteries of the spiritual life. Mary, Mother of Mercy, always faithful to Christ, lead me in the footsteps of the sorrowful Passion of your Son and ask for me the necessary graces for a fruitful making of this Way of the Cross.

Sung verse:

> At the cross her station keeping
> Stood the mournful Mother weeping
> Close to Jesus to the last

First Station: Jesus is condemned to die

Celebrant:

We adore You, O Christ, and we praise You.

People:

Because by Your holy Cross and Resurrection, You have redeemed the world.

Celebrant:

The chief priests and the entire Sanhedrin kept trying to obtain false testimony against Jesus in order to put Him to death, but they found none, though many false witnesses came forward (Matthew 26:59-60).

Jesus: (Celebrant)

Do not be surprised that you are sometimes unjustly accused. I Myself first drank this cup of undeserved suffering for love of you (289). When I was before Herod, I obtained a grace for you; namely, that you would be able to rise above human scorn and follow faithfully in My footsteps (1164).

S. Faustina: (People)

We are sensitive to words and quickly want to answer back, without taking any regard as to whether it is God's will that we should speak. A silent soul is strong; no adversities will harm it if it perseveres in silence. The silent soul is capable of attaining the closest union with God (477).

All:

Merciful Jesus, help me to know how to accept every human judgment and do not allow me ever to render a condemnatory judgment on You in my neighbours.

Celebrant:

You, who suffered wounds for us,

People:
Christ Jesus, have mercy on us.

Sung verse:
> Through her heart, His sorrow sharing
> All His bitter anguish bearing
> Now at length the sword has passed

Second Station: Jesus carries His cross
Celebrant:
We adore You, O Christ, and we praise You.

People:
Because by Your holy Cross and Resurrection, You have redeemed the world.

Celebrant:
Then Pilate took Jesus and had Him scourged. And the soldiers wove a crown out of thorns and placed it on His head, and clothed Him in a purple cloak, and they came to Him and said, "Hail, King of the Jews!"

So Jesus came out, wearing the crown of thorns and the purple cloak. And Pilate said to them, "Behold, the man!" When the chief priests and the guards saw Him they cried out, "Crucify Him, crucify Him!" (John 19:1-6).

Jesus: (Celebrant)
Do not be afraid of sufferings; I am with you (151). The more you will come to love suffering, the purer your love for Me will be (279).

S. Faustina: (People)
Jesus, I thank You for the little daily crosses, for opposition to my endeavours, for the hardships of communal life, for the misinterpretation of my intentions, for humiliations at the hands of

118

others, for the harsh way in which we are treated, for false suspicions, for poor health and loss of strength, for self-denial, for dying to myself, for lack of recognition in everything, for the upsetting of all my plans (343).

All:
Merciful Jesus, teach me to value life's toil, sicknesses, and every suffering, and with love to carry my daily crosses.

Celebrant:
You, who suffered wounds for us,

People:
Christ Jesus, have mercy on us.

Sung verse:
> O, how sad and sore distressed
> Was that Mother highly blessed
> of the sole Begotten One.

Third Station: Jesus falls the first time
Celebrant:
We adore You, O Christ, and we praise You.

People:
Because by Your holy Cross and Resurrection, You have redeemed the world.

Celebrant:
We had all gone astray like sheep, each following his own way; But the Lord laid upon Him the guilt of us all (Isaiah 53:6,12).

Jesus: (Celebrant)
Involuntary offences of souls do not hinder My love for them or prevent Me from uniting Myself with them. But voluntary

offences, even the smallest, obstruct My graces, and I cannot lavish My gifts on such souls (1641).

S. Faustina: (People)
My Jesus, despite Your graces, I see and feel all my misery...O my Jesus, how prone I am to evil, and this forces me to be constantly vigilant. But I do not lose heart. I trust God's grace, which abounds in the worst misery (606).

All:
Merciful Lord, preserve me from every, even the tiniest but voluntary and conscious infidelity.

Celebrant:
You, who suffered wounds for us,

People:
Christ Jesus, have mercy on us.

Sung verse:
> Is there one who would not weep,
> Whelmed in miseries so deep
> Christ's dear Mother to behold?

Fourth Station: Jesus meets His sorrowful mother
Celebrant:
We adore You, O Christ, and we praise You.

People:
Because by Your holy Cross and Resurrection, You have redeemed the world.

Celebrant:
Behold, this child is destined for the fall and rise of many in Israel, and to be a sign that will be contradicted so that the thoughts

of many hearts may be revealed. And you yourself a sword will pierce (Luke 2:34–35).

Jesus: (Celebrant)
Although all the works that come into being by My will are exposed to great sufferings, consider whether any of them has been subject to greater difficulties than that work which is directly Mine – the work of Redemption. You should not worry too much about adversities (1643).

S. Faustina: (People)
I saw the Blessed Virgin, unspeakably beautiful. She held me close to herself and said to me, I am Mother to you all, thanks to the unfathomable mercy of God. Most pleasing to me is that soul which faithfully carries out the will of God. Be courageous. Do not fear apparent obstacles, but fix your gaze upon the Passion of my Son, and in this way you will be victorious (449).

All:
Mary, Mother of Mercy, be near me always, especially in suffering as you were on your Son's Way of the Cross.

Celebrant:
You, who suffered wounds for us,

People:
Christ Jesus, have mercy on us.

Sung verse:
> Can the human heart refrain
> From partaking in her pain
> In that Mother's pain untold?

Fifth Station: Simon helps Jesus carry His cross

Celebrant:
We adore You, O Christ, and we praise You.

People:
Because by Your holy Cross and Resurrection, You have redeemed the world.

Celebrant:
As they led Him away they took hold of a certain Simon, a Cyrenian, who was coming in from the country; and after laying the cross on him, they made him carry it behind Jesus (Luke 23:26).

Jesus: (Celebrant)
Write that by day and by night My gaze is fixed upon him, and I permit these adversities in order to increase his merit. I do not reward for good results but for the patience and hardship undergone for My sake (86).

S. Faustina: (People)
Jesus, You do not give a reward for the successful performance of a work, but for the good will and the labour undertaken. Therefore, I am completely at peace, even if all my undertakings and efforts should be thwarted or should come to naught. If I do all that is in my power, the rest is not my business (952).

All:
Jesus, my Lord, let my every thought, word, and deed be undertaken exclusively out of love for You. Keep on cleansing my intentions.

Celebrant:
You, who suffered wounds for us,

People:
Christ Jesus, have mercy on us.

Sung verse:

> Let me share with thee His pain
> Who for all my sins was slain,
> Who for me in torments died.

Sixth Station: Veronica wipes the face of Jesus

Celebrant:
We adore You, O Christ, and we praise You.

People:
Because by Your holy Cross and Resurrection, You have redeemed the world.

Celebrant:
He grew up like a sapling before him, like a shoot from the parched Earth; There was in Him no stately bearing to make us look at Him, no appearance that would attract us to Him. He was spurned and avoided by men, a Man of suffering, accustomed to infirmity. One of those from whom men hide their faces spurned, and we held Him in no esteem (Isaiah 53:2-3).

Jesus: (Celebrant)
Know that whatever good you do to any soul, I accept it as if you had done it to Me (1768).

S. Faustina: (People)
I am learning how to be good from Jesus, from Him who is goodness itself, so that I may be called a [child] of the heavenly Father (669). Great love can change small things into great ones, and it is only love which lends value to our actions (303).

All:
Lord Jesus, my Master, grant that my eyes, my hands, my lips and my heart may always be merciful. Transform me into mercy.

Celebrant:
You, who suffered wounds for us,

People:
Christ Jesus, have mercy on us.

Sung verse:
> Let me mingle tears with thee,
> Mourning Him who mourned for me,
> All the days that I may live.

Seventh Station: Jesus falls the second time
Celebrant:
We adore You, O Christ, and we praise You.

People:
Because by Your holy Cross and Resurrection, You have redeemed the world.

Celebrant:
Yet it was our infirmities that He bore, our sufferings that He endured, while we thought of Him as stricken, as one smitten by God and afflicted (Isaiah 53:4).

Jesus: (Celebrant)
The cause of your falls is that you rely too much upon yourself and too little on Me. But let this not sadden you so much. You are dealing with the God of mercy (1488). Know that of yourself you can do nothing (639). Without special help from Me, you are not even capable of accepting My graces (738).

S. Faustina: (People)
Jesus, do not leave me alone in suffering. You know, Lord, how weak I am. I am an abyss of wretchedness, I am nothingness itself; so what will be so strange if You leave me alone and I fall? (1489). So

You, Jesus, must stand by me constantly like a mother by a helpless child – and even more so (264).

All:
May Your grace assist me, Lord, that I may not keep falling continuously into the same faults; and when I fall, help me to rise and glorify Your mercy.

Celebrant:
You, who suffered wounds for us,

People:
Christ Jesus, have mercy on us.

Sung verse:
> Make me feel as thou hast felt;
> Make my soul to glow and melt
> With the love of Christ my Lord

Eighth Station: Jesus meets the women of Jerusalem
Celebrant:
We adore You, O Christ, and we praise You.

People:
Because by Your holy Cross and Resurrection, You have redeemed the world.

Celebrant:
A large crowd of people followed Jesus, including many women who mourned and lamented Him. Jesus turned to them and said, "Daughters of Jerusalem, do not weep for Me; weep instead for yourselves and for your children (Luke 23:27-28).

Jesus: (Celebrant)
O how pleasing to Me is living faith! (1420). Tell all, that

I demand that they live in the spirit of faith (353).

S. Faustina: (People)
I fervently beg the Lord to strengthen my faith, so that in my drab, everyday life I will not be guided by human dispositions, but by those of the spirit. Oh, how everything drags Man towards the Earth! But lively faith maintains the soul in the higher regions and assigns self-love its proper place; that is to say, the lowest one (210).

All:
Merciful Lord, I thank You for holy Baptism and the grace of faith. Continuously, I call: Lord, I believe, increase my faith.

Celebrant:
You, who suffered wounds for us,

People:
Christ Jesus, have mercy on us.

Sung verse:
> O thou Mother! Fount of love!
> Touch my spirit from above,
> Make my heart with thine accord.

Ninth Station: Jesus falls the third time
Celebrant:
We adore You, O Christ, and we praise You.

People:
Because by Your holy Cross and Resurrection, You have redeemed the world.

Celebrant:
Though He was harshly treated, He submitted and opened not His mouth. Like a lamb led to the slaughter or a sheep before the

shearers, He was silent and opened not His mouth. Oppressed and condemned, though He had done no wrong nor spoken any falsehood. But the Lord was pleased to crush Him in infirmity. Because of His affliction He shall see the light in fulness of days (Isaiah 53:7-10).

Jesus: (Celebrant)
My child, know that the greatest obstacles to holiness are discouragement and an exaggerated anxiety. These will deprive you of the ability to practice virtue. Do not lose heart in coming for pardon, for I am always ready to forgive you. As often as you beg for it, you glorify My mercy (1488).

S. Faustina: (People)
My Jesus, despite Your graces, I see and feel all my misery. I begin my day with battle and end it with battle. As soon as I conquer one obstacle, ten more appear to take its place. But I am not worried, because I know that this is the time of struggle, not peace (606).

All:
Merciful Lord, I give over to You that which is my exclusive property, that is, my sin and my human weakness. I beg You, may my misery drown in Your unfathomable mercy.

Celebrant:
You, who suffered wounds for us,

People:
Christ Jesus, have mercy on us.

Sung verse:

> Wounded with His ev'ry wound
> Steep my soul till it hath swooned
> In His very Blood away.

127

Tenth Station: Jesus is stripped of His garments

Celebrant:
We adore You, O Christ, and we praise You.

People:
Because by Your holy Cross and Resurrection, You have redeemed the world.

Celebrant:
When the soldiers had crucified Jesus, they took His clothes and divided them into four shares, a share for each soldier. They also took His tunic, but the tunic was seamless, woven in one piece from the top down. So they said to one another, "Let's not tear it, but cast lots for it to see whose it will be," in order that the passage of scripture might be fulfilled (John 19:23-24).

S. Faustina: (People)
Jesus was suddenly standing before me, stripped of His clothes, His Body completely covered with wounds, His eyes flooded with tears and blood, His face disfigured and covered with spittle.

Jesus: (Celebrant)
The bride must resemble her betrothed.

S. Faustina: (People)
I understood these words to their very depth. There is no room for doubt here. My likeness to Jesus must be through suffering and humility (268).

All:
Jesus, meek and humble of heart, make my heart like unto Your heart.

Celebrant:
You, who suffered wounds for us,

People:

Christ Jesus, have mercy on us.

Sung verse:

> Bruised, derided, cursed, defiled,
> She beheld her tender Child
> All with bloody scourges rent

Eleventh Station: Jesus is nailed to the cross

Celebrant:

We adore You, O Christ, and we praise You.

People:

Because by Your holy Cross and Resurrection, You have redeemed the world.

Celebrant:

Those passing by reviled Him, shaking their heads and saying, "You would destroy the temple and rebuild it in three days, save Yourself, if You are the Son of God, [and] come down from the cross!" Likewise the chief priests with the scribes and elders mocked Him and said, "He saved others; He cannot save Himself. He trusted in God; let Him deliver Him now if he wants Him. For He said, 'I am the Son of God'" (Matthew 27:39-43).

Jesus: (Celebrant)

My pupil, have great love for those who cause you suffering. Do good to those who hate you (1628).

S. Faustina: (People)

O my Jesus, You know what efforts are needed to live sincerely and unaffectedly with those from whom our nature flees, or with those who, deliberately or not, have made us suffer. Humanly speaking, this is impossible. At such times more than at others, I try to discover the Lord Jesus in such a person and for the same

Jesus, I do everything for such people (766).

All:
O purest Love, rule in all Your plenitude in my heart and help me to do Your holy will most faithfully (328).

Celebrant:
You, who suffered wounds for us,

People:
Christ Jesus, have mercy on us.

Sung verse:
> Holy Mother! pierce me through;
> In my heart each wound renew
> Of my Saviour crucified.

Twelfth Station: Jesus dies on the cross
Celebrant:
We adore You, O Christ, and we praise You.

People:
Because by Your holy Cross and Resurrection, You have redeemed the world.

Celebrant:
But when they came to Jesus and saw that He was already dead, they did not break His legs, but one soldier thrust his lance into His side, and immediately blood and water flowed out (John 19:33–40).

Jesus: (Celebrant)
All this is for the salvation of souls. Consider well, My daughter, what you are doing for their salvation (1184).

S. Faustina: (People)

Then I saw the Lord Jesus nailed to the cross. When He had hung on it for a while, I saw a multitude of souls crucified like Him. Then I saw a second multitude of souls, and a third. The second multitude were not nailed to [their] crosses, but were holding them firmly in their hands. The third were neither nailed to [their] crosses nor holding them firmly in their hands, but were dragging [their] crosses behind them and were discontent.

Jesus: (Celebrant)

Do you see these souls? Those who are like Me in the pain and contempt they suffer will be like Me also in glory. And those who resemble Me less in pain and contempt will also bear less resemblance to Me in glory (446).

All:

Jesus, my Saviour, hide me in the depth of Your heart that, fortified by Your grace, I may be able to resemble You in the love of the Cross and have a share in Your glory.

Celebrant:

You, who suffered wounds for us,

People:

Christ Jesus, have mercy on us.

Sung verse:

> For the sins of His own nation,
> Saw Him hang in desolation
> Till His Spirit forth He sent

Thirteenth Station: Jesus is taken down from the cross
Celebrant:

We adore You, O Christ, and we praise You.

People:
Because by Your holy Cross and Resurrection, You have redeemed the world.

Celebrant:
The centurion who witnessed what had happened glorified God and said, "This man was innocent beyond doubt." When all the people who had gathered for this spectacle saw what had happened, they returned home beating their breasts; but all His acquaintances stood at a distance, including the women who had followed Him from Galilee, and saw these events (Luke 23:47-49).

Jesus: (Celebrant)
Most dear to Me is the soul that strongly believes in My goodness and has complete trust in Me. I heap My confidence upon it and give it all it asks (453).

S. Faustina: (People)
I fly to Your mercy, Compassionate God, who alone are good. Although my misery is great, and my offenses are many, I trust in Your mercy, because You are the God of mercy; and, from time immemorial, it has never been heard of, nor do heaven or earth remember, that a soul trusting in Your mercy has been disappointed (1730).

All:
Merciful Jesus, daily increase my trust in Your mercy that always and everywhere I may give witness to Your boundless goodness and love.

Celebrant:
You, who suffered wounds for us,

People:
Christ Jesus, have mercy on us.

Sung verse:

> Virgin of all virgins blest!
>
> Listen to my fond request:
>
> Let me share your grief divine

Fourteenth Station: Jesus is placed in the sepulchre

Celebrant:

We adore You, O Christ, and we praise You.

People:

Because by Your holy Cross and Resurrection, You have redeemed the world.

Celebrant:

They took the Body of Jesus and bound It with burial cloths along with the spices, according to the Jewish burial custom. Now in the place where He had been crucified there was a garden, and in the garden a new tomb, in which no one had yet been buried. So they laid Jesus there because of the Jewish preparation day; for the tomb was close by (John 19:38–42).

Jesus: (Celebrant)

But child, you are not yet in your homeland; so go, fortified by My grace, and fight for My kingdom in human souls; fight as a king's child would; and remember that the days of your exile will pass quickly, and with them the possibility of earning merit for heaven. I expect from you, My child, a great number of souls who will glorify My mercy for all eternity (1489).

S. Faustina: (People)

Every soul You have entrusted to me, Jesus, I will try to aid with prayer and sacrifice, so that Your grace can work in them. O great lover of souls, my Jesus, I thank You for this immense confidence with which You have deigned to place souls in our care (245).

All:

Grant, Merciful Lord, that not even one of those souls which You have entrusted to me be lost.

Celebrant:

You, who suffered wounds for us,

People:

Christ Jesus, have mercy on us.

Sung verse:

> Christ, when Thou shalt call me hence,
> Be Thy Mother my defence,
> Be Thy Cross my victory

All:

My Jesus, my only hope, I thank You for this book which You opened to the eyes of my soul. This book is Your Passion, undertaken out of love for me. From this book, I learn how to love God and souls. This book contains inexhaustible treasures. O Jesus, how few souls understand You in Your martyrdom of love. Happy the soul that has come to understand the love of the heart of Jesus!

For the intentions of the Holy Father

Our Father…Hail Mary…Glory Be…

Prayer in Honor of the Holy Cross:

God our Father, in obedience to You Your only Son accepted death on the cross for the salvation of mankind. We acknowledge the mystery of the cross on earth. May we receive the gift of redemption in Heaven. We ask this through our Lord Jesus Christ, Your Son, Who lives and reigns with You and the Holy Spirit one God, for ever and ever. Amen.

(Sung verses taken from the hymn, *Stabat Mater*)

Prayers that will be beneficial during The Hour of Mercy

The Fifteen Prayers Revealed by Our Lord to St Bridget of Sweden in the Church of St Paul, Rome

As St Bridget knelt before the Crucifix, above the Tabernacle in the Blessed Sacrament Chapel, she received fifteen prayers from Our Lord Jesus Christ. The crucifix is still displayed in the Church of St Paul in Rome. The inscription placed in the Church reads as follows: "Pendentis pendent Dei verba accepitaure accipit at verbum corde Brigitta Deum. Anno Junilei MCCCCL" which recalls the mystery of the crucifix conversing with St Bridget. "Bridget not only receives the words of God hanging in the air, but takes the Word of God into her heart. Jubilee Year 1350."

The Prayers will be extremely useful as a basis for meditation during the Hour of Mercy.

Pope Pius IX approved the prayers on 31st May 1862, as true and for the good of souls.

First Prayer

Our Father – Hail Mary. O Jesus Christ! Eternal Sweetness to those who love You, joy surpassing all joy and all desire, salvation and hope of all sinners, You have proved that You have no greater desire than to be among men, even assuming human nature at the fulness of time for the love of men, recall all the sufferings You have endured from the instant of Your conception, and especially during Your Passion, as it was decreed and ordained from all eternity in the Divine plan.

Remember, O Lord, that during the Last Supper with Your disciples, having washed their feet, You gave them Your Most Precious Body and Blood, and while at the same time You did sweetly console them, You did foretell of Your coming Passion.

Remember, the sadness and bitterness which You did experience in Your Soul as You Yourself bore witness saying: "My Soul is sorrowful even unto death."

Remember all the fear, anguish and pain that You did suffer in Your delicate Body before the torment of the Crucifixion, when, after having prayed three times, bathed in a sweat of blood, You were betrayed by Judas, Your disciple, arrested by the people of a nation You had chosen and elevated, accused by false witnesses, unjustly judged by their judges during the flower of Your youth and during the solemn paschal season.

Remember that You were despoiled of Your garments and clothed in those of derision; that Your Face and Eyes were veiled, that You were buffeted, crowned with thorns, a reed placed in Your Hands, that You were crushed with blows and overwhelmed with affronts and outrages.

In memory of all these pains and sufferings which You did endure before Your Passion on the Cross, grant me before my death true contrition, a sincere and entire confession, worthy satisfaction and the remission of all my sins. Amen.

Second Prayer

Our Father – Hail Mary. O Jesus! True liberty of angels, Paradise of delights, remember the horror and sadness which You did endure when Your enemies, like furious lions, surrounded You, and by thousands of insults, spits, blows, lacerations and other unheard-of cruelties, tormented You at will. In consideration of these torments and insulting words, I beseech You, O my Saviour, to deliver me from all my enemies visible and invisible and to bring me, under Your protection, to the perfection of eternal salvation, Amen.

Third Prayer

Our Father – Hail Mary. O Jesus! Creator of Heaven and Earth Whom nothing can encompass or limit, You Who do enfold and hold all under Your Loving power, remember the very bitter pain You did suffer when the Jews nailed Your Sacred Hands and Feet to the Cross by blow after blow with big blunt nails, and not finding

You in a pitiable enough state to satisfy their rage, they enlarged Your Wounds, and added pain to pain, and with indescribable cruelty stretched Your Body on the Cross, pulled You from all sides, thus dislocating Your Limbs. I beg of You, O Jesus, by the memory of this most loving suffering of the Cross, to grant me the grace to fear You and to Love You. Amen.

Fourth Prayer

Our Father – Hail Mary. O Jesus! Heavenly Physician, raised aloft on the Cross to heal our wounds with Yours, remember the bruises which You did suffer and the weakness of all Your members which were distended to such a degree that never was there pain like Yours. From the crown on your Head to the Soles of Your Feet there was not one spot on Your Body that was not in torment, and yet, forgetting all Your sufferings, You did not cease to pray to Your Heavenly Father for Your enemies saying: "Father forgive them for they know not what they do."

Through this great Mercy, and in memory of this suffering, grant that the remembrance of Your Most Bitter Passion may effect in us a perfect contrition and the remission of all our sins. Amen.

Fifth Prayer

Our Father – Hail Mary. O Jesus! Mirror of eternal splendour, remember the sadness which You experienced, when contemplating in the light of Your Divinity and predestination of those who would be saved by the merits of Your Sacred Passion, You did see at the same time, the great multitude of reprobates who would be damned for their sins, and You did complain bitterly of those hopeless lost and unfortunate sinners. Through this abyss of compassion and pity, and especially through the goodness which You displayed to the good thief when You said to him: "This day, You shall be with Me in Paradise." I beg of You, O Sweet Jesus, that at the hour of my death, You will show me mercy too. Amen.

Sixth Prayer

Our Father – Hail Mary. O Jesus! Beloved and most desirable King, remember the grief You did suffer, when naked and like a common criminal, You were fastened and raised on the Cross, when all Your relatives and friends abandoned You, except Your Beloved Mother, who remained close to You during Your agony and whom You did entrust to Your faithful disciple when You said to Mary: "Woman, behold your son!" And to St John: "Son, behold Your Mother!"

I beg of You O my Saviour, by the sword of sorrow which pierced the soul of Your holy Mother, to have compassion on me in all my afflictions and tribulations, both corporal and spiritual, and to assist me in all my trials, and especially at the hour of my death. Amen.

Seventh Prayer

Our Father – Hail Mary. O Jesus! Inexhaustible Fountain of compassion, Who by a profound gesture of Love, said from the Cross: "I thirst", suffered with a thirst for the salvation of the human race. I beg of You O my Saviour, to inflame in our hearts the desire to tend towards perfection in all our acts; and to extinguish in us the excessive desire of the flesh and the love of worldly things. Amen.

Eighth Prayer

Our Father – Hail Mary. O Jesus! Sweetness of Hearts, delight of the spirit, by the bitterness of the vinegar and gall which You did taste on the Cross for Love of us, grant us the grace to receive worthily Your Precious Body and Blood during our life and at the hour of our death, that they may serve as a remedy and consolation for our souls. Amen.

Ninth Prayer

Our Father – Hail Mary. O Jesus! Royal virtue, joy of the mind, recall the pain You did endure when, plunged in an ocean of bitterness at the approach of death, insulted and outraged, You did cry out in a loud voice that You were abandoned by Your Father, saying "My God, My God, why hast thou forsaken me? Through this anguish, I beg of You, O my Saviour, not to abandon me in the terrors and pains of my death. Amen.

Tenth Prayer

Our Father – Hail Mary. O Jesus! Who art the beginning and end of all things, life and virtue, remember that for our sakes You were plunged in an abyss of suffering from the soles of Your Feet to the crown of Your Head. In consideration of the enormity of Your Wounds, teach me to keep, through pure love, Your Commandments, whose way are wide and easy for those who love you. Amen.

Eleventh Prayer

Our Father – Hail Mary. O Jesus! Deep abyss of mercy, I beg of You, in memory of Your Wounds which penetrated to the very marrow of Your Bones and to the depth of Your Being, to draw me, a miserable sinner, overwhelmed by my offences, away from sin and to hide me from Your Face, justly irritated against me, hide me in Your Wounds, until Your anger and just indignation shall have passed away. Amen.

Twelfth Prayer

Our Father – Hail Mary. O Jesus! Mirror of Truth, Symbol of Unity, Link of Charity, remember the multitude of wounds with which You were covered from head to foot, torn and reddened by the spilling of Your adorable Blood. O Great and Universal Pain which You did suffer in Your virginal Flesh for Love of us! Sweetest Jesus! What is there that You could have done for us which You have not done? May the fruit of Your sufferings be renewed in my soul by the faithful remembrance of Your Passion and may Your Love increase in my heart each day, until I see You in eternity.

You who are the treasury of every real good and every joy, which I beg You to grant me, O Sweetest Jesus, in Heaven, Amen.

Thirteenth Prayer

Our Father – Hail Mary. O Jesus! Strong Lion, Immortal and Invincible King, remember the pain which You did endure when all Your strength, both moral and physical, was entirely exhausted, You did bow Your Head, saying: "It is consummated." Through this anguish and grief, I beg of You Lord Jesus, to have mercy on me at the hour of my death when my mind will be greatly troubled and my soul will be in anguish. Amen.

Fourteenth Prayer
Our Father – Hail Mary. O Jesus! Only Son of the Father, Splendour and Figure of His Substance, remember the simple and humble recommendation You did make of Your Soul to Your Eternal Father, saying: "Father, into Your Hands I commend my Spirit!" And with Your Body all torn, and Your Heart broken, and the bowels of Your Mercy open to redeem us, You did Expire. By this Precious Death, I beg of You O King of Saints, comfort me and help me to resist the Devil, the flesh and the world, so that being dead to the world I may live for You alone. I beg of You at the hour of my death to receive me, a pilgrim and an exile returning to You. Amen.

Fifteenth Prayer
Our Father – Hail Mary. O Jesus! True and fruitful Vine! Remember the abundant outpouring of Blood which You did so generously shed from Your Sacred Body as juice from grapes in a wine press. From Your Side, pierced with a lance by a soldier, blood and water issued forth until there was not left in Your Body a single drop, and finally, like a bundle of myrrh lifted to the top of the Cross your delicate Flesh was destroyed, the very Substance of Your Body withered, and the Marrow of Your Bones dried up. Through this bitter Passion and through the outpouring of Your Precious Blood, I beg of You, O Sweet Jesus, to receive my soul when I am in my death agony. Amen.

Conclusion
O Sweet Jesus! Pierce my heart so that my tears of penitence and love will be my bread day and night; may I be converted entirely to You, may my heart be Your perpetual habitation, may my conversation be pleasing to You, and may the end of my life be so praiseworthy that

I may merit Heaven and there with Your saints, praise You forever. Amen.

The spread of the Divine Mercy Devotion

Jesus said: "Do whatever is within your power to spread devotion to My mercy. I will make up for what you lack. (Diary 1074)

"Souls who spread the honour of My mercy I shield through their entire lives as a tender mother her Infant, and at the hour of death I will not be a Judge for them, but the Merciful Saviour." (Diary 1075) Christ promised to Saint Faustina that those who spread the devotion would be given graces and assistance at the hour of death.

CHAPTER 3

The Great Devotions

Devotion to the Sacred Heart

The use of the heart of flesh of Jesus as the sensible object of this devotion has a scriptural foundation. In the Old Testament, the inspired writers use the heart as the place where God sees all human actions, their motives and their sincerity. It is in the heart that the writers believe that God has planted his unwritten law and where God sees whether human beings are reacting to his laws. So, in a mysterious way, it is in the heart that man meets God's love and God sees in man how he responds to that love. A wicked heart is the heart that turns away from God but that heart can return to God when he shows contrition and thus comes with a new heart (Psalm 51). It is the man with a pure heart who sees God (Matt. 5:8). And so the Psalmist also says: "Their hearts are astray, these people do not know my ways." St Augustine states that no one will be fit to see God in the kingdom of Heaven unless he has prepared himself in this life with a pure heart to see God. He states as follows: "For if you never turn aside from a holy life, though your tongue is silent your life speaks aloud; God has ears for what your heart is saying." This saint believes that because God has planted his unwritten law in our hearts, man will become restless until he finds God.

In the New Testament, Christ makes of His heart of flesh, the symbol and reality. Foretelling His approaching death in St John's gospel, He cried out as follows: "Let anyone who believes in Me come and drink! As scripture says, 'From his heart shall flow streams of living water.'" (John 7: 37-38). When therefore, blood and water flowed from His pierced side on the cross, it was clear that the blood and water was flowing from the heart. It was therefore from the heart of Jesus that the water of baptism and the blood of our redemption came. Jesus confirms this spiritual truth to Saint Faustina as follows: "My Heart overflows with great mercy for souls, and especially for poor sinners. If only they could understand that I am the best of Fathers to them and that it is for them that Blood and Water flowed from My Heart as from a fount overflowing with mercy. For them I dwell in the tabernacle as King of Mercy. I desire to bestow My graces upon souls, but they do not want to accept them." (Diary 367)

Let us remember that Christ ascended into heaven with his glorified Body which includes His heart of flesh. It is this pierced heart which becomes our permanent blood and water of redemption, the source of all mercies and graces for mankind. The redemptive action of the heart will continue to send to humanity the gifts necessary for our redemption.

Sacred Heart Devotion as revealed to Saint Margaret Mary Alacoque

Saint Margaret Mary revealed the revelation to Blessed Claude de la Colombiere as follows: "Being one day before the Blessed Sacrament during the Octave of the Feast, I received from my God excessive graces of His love. When I was moved by the desire to make some return to Him and to render love for love, He said to me: 'You can give Me no greater return than by doing what I have so many times commanded you to do,' and revealing His Heart to me He said: 'Behold this Heart which has so loved men as to spare Itself nothing, even to exhausting and consuming Itself, to testify to them Its love, and in return I receive nothing but ingratitude from the greater part of men by the contempt, irreverence, sacrileges, and coldness which they have for Me in this Sacrament of My love; but what is still more painful is that it is hearts consecrated to Me that treat Me thus. For this reason I ask that the First Friday after the Octave of Corpus Christi be set apart for a particular feast to honour My Heart; I ask that reparation of honour be made to My Heart; that Communion be received on that day to repair the indignities which It has received during the time It has been exposed on the altars; and I promise you that My Heart will expand Itself and pour out in abundance the influences of its love on those who will render it this honour.'

The Sacred Heart Devotion should therefore be considered as a merciful act of Christ which gives mankind the opportunity to show our love for him and to recall to our own hearts the sacrifices which Christ undertook for our redemption by enduring humiliations, torture and crucifixion. All these sacrifices, He undertook to save mankind from the eternal death to which Satan was dragging us.

The devotion to the Sacred Heart is also linked inseparably to His love for us expressed in His gift of the Blessed Sacrament of the Eucharist. He confirms to us that the bread and wine used in the sacrifice of the Holy Mass are consecrated to become the Body and Blood of His Passion which He underwent to atone for the sins of the world, to console His Father and increase His glory. So, in the Blessed Sacrament, Christ actually gives to us all the merits of His earthly sacrifice to atone for our sins and enables us to share in His divinity and lead us to eternal life.

The devotion to the Sacred Heart as an act of reparation

The devotion to the Sacred Heart has been seen principally as an act of reparation by the faithful followers of Christ who sincerely loved Him and are expressing sorrow, looking at His heart, at the way that He was treated by mankind on the cross and continues to be treated even in our day by men who show no gratitude for His sacrifice and live as though they have not been redeemed. So in making the devotion, we must focus on making a reparation of honour to Christ for the indignities which He suffered for our redemption, while lamenting inwardly that people are either ignorant of His love or they have no time for the serious question of redemption. In making reparations, we must accept our crosses for love of God and offer these crosses in atonement for our sins and those of the whole world. By our acceptance of our crosses through the Sacred Heart Devotions, our journey in this life becomes a source of joy and peace, devoid of all bitterness because we are united with Christ through the supernatural graces of the Holy Spirit. "If any man will come after me, let him deny himself and take up his cross daily, and follow Me." (Luke 9:23)

The Twelve Promises of the Sacred Heart

Introduction

According to the testimony of Saint Margaret Mary Alacoque, Our Lord promised special rewards and graces to those who practise the devotion to the Sacred Heart. The reason underlying the promise is that, according to the saint, "the Heart of Jesus contains the treasures of grace, and it is the Saviour's will to pour them forth on men through the medium of devotion to this Sacred Heart." The twelve promises give assurances of exceptional personal blessings, both spiritual and temporal. Therefore we have endeavoured to attach to each promise their meaning, value and importance. Christ appreciates that Christians of all states of life, whether priest, religious or laity are confronted not only with the duties of their daily lives but are also confronted with spiritual warfare against Satan and forces of darkness. They therefore need graces to give light to the mind and the will to enable them to avoid evil and do good. These promises will therefore provide the essential graces necessary for salvation and for perfect souls extraordinary graces which will lead even to greater perfection.

The First Promise

"I will give them all the graces necessary for their state of life."

To be able to obtain these graces, we need prayer and the sacraments which the devotion to the Sacred Heart will enable us to fulfil. Thus, for married people, the devotion will help them in their marriage state. We would be assured through this promise that as and when necessary, the seven sacraments will help us to obtain salvation. In addition, God in his extra-ordinary providence will give us the graces which are of a powerful and efficacious kind.

The Second Promise

"I will give peace in their families."

Here Christ promises to give us true peace which can only be achieved through the subordination of our will to the will of God who is the source of true peace. The peace of the world is found in sensual enjoyment and in the gratification of the passions, in riches, honours and pride but all these lead to disappointment, death and everlasting misery but the peace of God brings interior peace. Within the family, the peace of the world leads to discord, bitterness and unkind words and brings about acrimony between wife and husband and between children and parents. The peace of God brings about forgetfulness of self, self-sacrifice, and self-restraint. The devotion to the Sacred Heart can be the foundation of the peace of God which will bring love in the family circle.

The Third Promise

"I will console them in all their troubles."

The heart of Jesus, being human and divine is here portrayed as generous and noble with the generosity of God Himself. After all God's love was shown in the life of Jesus who showed compassion to all men. At the ascension, He promised to be with us and to console us until the end of time. Moreover, He gives His body and blood of love to us in the Eucharist. So this Heart of Christ continues to give comfort and consolation to all who bear various burdens of life. The third promise brings us the full sympathy of Christ who has suffered Himself on the cross. He will help us in our struggle as we deal with the world and its dangerous attractions and to attain eternal life. He will console us as He consoles his Blessed Mother, the apostles and the saints. He will ensure us of His comfort as we struggle through sufferings to be chastened and He will use the sufferings to detach us from the things of this world and raise our hearts and minds to our heavenly goal.

The Fourth Promise

"They shall find in My Heart an assured refuge during life and especially at the hour of death."

On the cross, the Roman soldier pierced the side of Jesus and blood and water came out. Saint Bernard said that the heart was opened in order to make the heart a refuge for mankind. So his belief was that it was God's will that the heart should be pierced. During our lifetime and at the hour of death, the Sacred Heart is our refuge against our weaknesses and all that strives within us for our ruin. The Heart of Jesus is the refuge where poor, weak human nature finds the strength and energy and grace to fight against itself and overcome its misery and inclination to all evil. The Heart of Jesus is also a refuge against our exterior enemies, the world and the Devil. Against their attacks, we need an assured refuge. Thirdly, the Sacred Heart is our refuge against God's avenging justice. St Margaret Mary writes: "Never be tired of recommending devotion to the Sacred Heart; it is through it that God works to save many souls from everlasting death. This Divine Heart is an assured refuge against God's just anger towards sinners."

The Sacred Heart is also our refuge, especially at the hour of death. When people tremble at the thought of approaching judgement and the eternal issues that depend on it, the Sacred Heart of love becomes their comfort and the sweet mercies of the crucified Redeemer. It will be the consolation of Christ who is ever faithful to what He has promised.

The Fifth Promise

"I will pour abundant blessings on all their enterprises."

Here we must remember that God's providence is not to be viewed as referring to our temporal and material interest but what God knows is good for our highest welfare. Our prayers are answered if offered with good dispositions and with the intention of seeking our true end. God does not answer prayers if they will lead to our eternal ruin or obstruct our attaining our salvation. Those who cultivate a sincere devotion to the Sacred Heart must seek God's providence and protection and must view all material things as opportunities to honour God through service of their neighbour. In this way, they will experience the blessing of Heaven in all their enterprises, according to what Jesus told St Margaret Mary.

The Sixth Promise

"Sinners shall find in My Heart the source and infinite ocean of mercy."

God's mercy has been at work since creating Man out of nothing. He created us in His own image and likeness and put Man at the summit of creation and gave us a share in his kingdom with the supernatural destiny. However, it was in Christ Jesus, the Redeemer who through His incarnation, God showed His boundless mercy for mankind. When man lost his birthright by the fall of our first parents, God did not cast us away to eternal death but sent His son to redeem mankind. This act of God's mercy comes from His love and this love is manifested in the Sacred Heart of Jesus because it was that Heart of Love that prompted all the endless acts of tender mercy that were manifested in our Lord's life on earth. In His Eucharistic life upon our altars, the Heart of Jesus is the source of His boundless mercy, to which sinners may turn with absolute confidence that their cry of heartfelt repentance will be heard and win them pardon. The Divine Heart also appeases the anger of Divine Justice which our sins have aroused. The Sacred Heart is to establish God's reign in our midst, granting us graces of sanctification and salvation.

The Seventh Promise

"Tepid souls shall become fervent."

The tepid soul is a person who has no fear whatever. They are quite at ease with their tepidity because they do not care about their real state of spiritual destitution. These are souls that have all but lost their grip of the supernatural and therefore do not know or fear the danger they are in. They pray without attention, they go to confession without any attempt at amendment. They go to Communion without fruit. They dislike spiritual things. Their venial sins are multiplied but they have no anxiety and they are gradually led into spiritual death. In this condition, they fall an easy prey to the promptings of the Devil and their nature becomes corrupted.

True devotion to the Sacred Heart can cure this condition. It can develop in us the humble trust and confidence in God's love and protection and gradually tepid souls become fervent. They must believe that by honouring the Sacred Heart and placing themselves under its protection, they will be restored to God's favour.

The Eighth Promise
"Fervent souls shall speedily rise to great perfection."

Here, we are talking about how through the devotion to the Sacred Heart, Christ can bestow on us a close resemblance to Himself and kindle in our souls a fire of divine love. The devotion will give us strength and courage from the thought of Christ and His saints and give us comfort that leads to holiness. It will inspire in us the love of God and of our neighbour for His sake. It will instil in us self-sacrifice and remove the obstacles to the full reign of Christ in the soul. In this way, we shall no longer wish for anything except in accordance with God's will. We shall also in the devotion seek God's light and direction and give Him glory of everything looking upon ourselves as totally dependent on Him and His providence. So through the devotion to the Sacred Heart, we become entirely and intimately united to our Lord. In short, the Sacred Heart has in it the graces capable of leading the devotees rapidly to very high perfection.

The Ninth Promise
"I will bless the homes in which the image of My Heart shall be exposed and honoured."

Here Christ assured Saint Margaret Mary that He took a singular delight in being honoured under the figure of His heart of flesh in homes, in churches and even in public places. However, we must remember that the image is to be honoured for the sake of Christ which the image represents and people who look at the image are to be lifted to the memory and love of the saving heart of Jesus. We must think of the Sacred Heart through the image as bringing us special graces and blessings that Christ Himself has promised.

In looking at the image, we must reflect on the Heart of Flesh of Jesus which is still in His glorified Body which is a source of grace for all fervent souls. It must remind us to follow the love of the heart for our neighbour and our duty to work for the glory of God. We must reflect on the thorns that still pierce the Heart of Jesus because of our sins, faults and negligence and the disrespect of many Christians for the Eucharist. The image of the Heart should inspire us to bear our crosses with Christ.

The Tenth Promise

"I will give to priests the power to touch the most hardened hearts."

This promise is addressed to priests and it offers special assistance to priests who labour for the salvation of souls. The devotion will help them to achieve extraordinary successes in their work. It will show them how to win souls to God and bring special graces on the work for souls that they have undertaken. They will have the supernatural help that is needed to convert hardened souls.

The Eleventh Promise

"Those who propagate this Devotion shall have their name written in My Heart, and it shall never be effaced."

This is a promise to those who promote devotion to the Sacred Heart. These souls are devout and they have consecrated themselves, their thoughts, words, sufferings and labours to the service of the Sacred Heart. By their actions, they have won the strong and faithful friendship of Christ and they have a special love. By having their names written in the Heart of Jesus, they have an assurance of final perseverance and salvation.

The Twelfth Promise: "The Great Promise"

"I promise thee in the excess of the mercy of My Heart, that its all-powerful love will grant to all those who shall receive Communion on the first Friday of nine consecutive months the grace of final repentance; they shall not die under My displeasure, nor without receiving their sacraments; My divine heart shall be their assured refuge at that last hour."

The phrases "excess of mercy" and "all-powerful love" are remarkable and suggest something very exceptional in the nature of the promise. Such grace is neither merited nor given as an acquired right, but purely out of God's "excess of mercy". As St Theresa of Lisieux said, God distributes his graces to whom He wills and when He wills. The condition for receiving the graces is the reception of Holy Communion, with proper dispositions, in honour of the Sacred Heart on first Fridays of nine consecutive months. The favour expected is the final grace of repentance and a happy death and blessed eternity. Where a person receives a sudden death without the last sacrament, he still receives the favour because God may foresee that for certain persons, an ordinary death would prove dangerous to salvation, such as temptation on the bed of death.

Novena to the Sacred Heart of Jesus

First Day

God Our Father, as we prepare ourselves for the feast of the Sacred Heart of Jesus, Your Son, we beg You to remove from our minds all darkness, so as to enable us, by the light of Your Holy Spirit, to understand the wonderful gifts of mercy that are pouring on mankind through the heart of Jesus. Father, You created us in love for Yourself and it was Your wish that we share Your divinity. We thank You that even when we sin, You did not abandon Your purpose for mankind but through the sacrifice of Your Son, You called us through Your mercy to a new life in the kingdom of Heaven. By the institution of the Heart of Jesus, You have shown us the centre of Your love for mankind and You pour through that heart all the graces necessary for redemption. As we prepare for the feast of the heart of Your Son, bless all those who seek Your mercies through this devotion and bring them to true repentance through reparation for their sins and contempt for the Devil, the world and the flesh. May the reign of the Heart of Jesus and the Immaculate Heart of Mary cleanse all faithful souls from their sins and lead them to eternal life.

Second Day

Lord Jesus Christ, through the cross, You gave all Your life to mankind and You showed this love through the gift of the Eucharist. We are sorry that through the frequent reception of the Eucharist, we have failed to reflect on the meaning of Your gift and we have also failed to ensure that we receive this gift worthily. As we contemplate the Heart of Jesus and the gifts that Your pierced heart continues to pour gifts on mankind, we beg You to infuse into our souls through repentance for all the offences we have committed against Your heart of love.

Most Sacred Heart of Jesus, we place all our trust in You.

Third Day

Oh Sacred Heart of Jesus, we pray that all families will contemplate the image of Your heart and reflect on the Heart of Jesus as the true source of peace in families. Through devotion to the Heart of Jesus, may we submit fully to the will of God the Father, our Creator, so that we may find true peace and harmony in our families. We are sorry that we have marginalized the commandments of God and look for happiness from riches, worldly honours and pride. Through the Heart of Jesus, may we have the eyes to see that the pleasures and ambitions of this world have led families and neighbours to gossip, bitterness, power struggles, hatred, which have all put people on the road to eternal death.

Oh Heart of Jesus, may we have time to listen to Your interior voice which will lead us to true peace in our own hearts and help us to lead the kind of lives that will unite our hearts to Your Heart. May the Holy Family of Nazareth be a model for all families to imitate. May they see the simplicity of Saint Joseph who found riches in doing God's will and protecting the vulnerable God-child. May families also behold the humility of the Blessed Virgin Mary whose only joy was being united to her Son in body and soul. Finally, we thank God for giving us a Son in human form and presenting Him as a model of a child obedient to His parents and Whose heart became the source of true peace in the family.

Fourth Day

Sacred Heart of Jesus, pierced with a spear to pour on mankind the gifts of the water, of the spirit and the blood of redemption and to atone for our sins, help us in our moments of temptations and trials, to learn how to bear our crosses. May we find consolation in the Heart of Jesus whenever we go through trials and temptations. May the outpouring of graces from Your Sacred Heart inspire us with the same feelings and thoughts which strengthen You, in obedience to the Father, to suffer humiliation and death on the cross. Oh Heart of Jesus, bless us so that our sorrows may serve as means to chasten us and detach us from the pleasures of this world. Oh Sweet Jesus, on the cross, You forgave us our sins and through the sacrament of penance, You forgive us when we sin. Through Your perfect example of love and forgiveness, grant us Your healing so that our crosses may not lead us to bitterness and hatred but rather to sweetness, joy and peace.

Fifth Day

Oh Sweet Jesus, in our most difficult moments, Your Heart is our safest refuge. Our most difficult moments will be the end of our lives when we face the just judgment of God. As God is infinitely good, we can never do enough to appease Him for our offences against him. So, Heart of Jesus, Be our safe refuge at the terrible moments of God's judgments at the hour of our deaths. Heart of Jesus, we pray for all souls to sincerely repent of their sins before their death and prepare themselves to be in the state to take refuge in Your heart as the truest preparation for death. Oh Sacred Heart of Jesus, we place all our trust in You.

Sixth Day

Oh Heart of Jesus, bless all persons in whatever occupations they are engaged in, at workplaces, entertainment, sports and social functions. May the Heart of Jesus be present even when we seek our material interest so that infused with the gifts of the spirit, we may use them for God's purpose for the good of others and help us on the road to salvation. May God keep away from us material things that may ruin our eternal salvation and give us only what will promote our eternal good and may we learn to hold in contempt, passing fortunes and pleasures that lead to damnation.

Oh Sacred Heart of Jesus, protect and watch over our harmful desires.

Seventh Day

Oh Heart of Jesus, Your gifts are constantly pouring out on all who have the heart to receive these gifts. Infused in our hearts is the desire to receive the gifts pouring from Your Heart but as we cannot receive supernatural things without giving ourselves time for reflection, we pray for the gift of recollection so that we may have time to think of the shortness of our lives and how we should use our short lives to prepare for our salvation and that of the whole world. We invoke God's mercy to give us the gifts through Your Heart so that all mankind will have time for reflection on the things they have done that darken the soul and prevent them from receiving the gifts of God's spirit. Oh Sacred Heart of Jesus, rescue us from our wretchedness so that we may have time to think of our true end which is in God.

Eighth Day

Oh Heart of Jesus, You are our safe refuge but we live in various forms of misery because we have not trusted in Your mercy flowing from Your Heart. We have put ourselves in our various forms of misery because we have yielded to the whispering of the Devil who convinces us that nothing can be done about our spiritual states in which we find ourselves. Many refuse to know or think about their state of spiritual misery. They refuse to think of purgatory or hell because they have lost grip of supernatural things in the mystery of redemption. Others go to confessions without any real intention to remove themselves from the repeat sins which they commit. Others also receive the Holy Communion without any reverence towards what is truly the Body of Christ Himself. All these miserable persons live in a state of coldness, ingratitude and contempt.

Oh Sacred Heart of Jesus, from the graces pouring from Your Heart, transform us into new persons. Give us the courage and determination through prayer and sacrifice to remove all the obstacles to our perfection so that through devotion to Your Heart, our hearts may be united to Your Heart, to love holiness that will make us the true children of God.

Ninth Day

Oh Heart of Jesus, we thank You for the gifts that we have received from Your Heart by faithfully praying to Your Heart during this novena. We have prayed the novena united in spirit to the assembly of God's people, the Body of Christ. May Your Heart reign in the Hearts of all the people of God, our Holy Father the Pope, the hierarchy of the Church, priests and religious. May the Heart of Jesus protect the faithful consecrated to God's service so that they may be true and faithful witnesses to the Gospel and make sacrifices for the salvation of souls. May they lead the faithful in the devotion to the Heart of Jesus, the source of all the gifts necessary for salvation. May they believe and practice true devotion to the Heart of Jesus and may they know that the greatest works of God can only be accomplished through the Heart of Jesus.

Oh Sacred Heart of Jesus, we place all our trust in You. May Your kingdom come.

Act of Consecration to the Sacred Heart of Our Lord Jesus Christ

O Lord Jesus, holy and sweet love of our souls who has promised that wherever two or three are gathered together in Your name, You will be there in their midst, behold, O Divine and most amiable Jesus, our hearts united in one common accord to adore, praise, love, bless and please Your most Holy and Sacred Heart, to which we dedicate ourselves and consecrate our hearts for time and eternity. We renounce forever all love and affection which are not in the love and affection of Your adorable Heart; we desire that all the desires, longings and aspirations of our hearts may be always according to the good pleasure of Your Heart, which we wish to please as much as we are able. But as we can do nothing good of ourselves, we beg You, O most adorable Jesus, by the infinite goodness and meekness of Your most Sacred Heart, to sustain our hearts and confirm them in the resolution of loving and serving You, with which You inspire them in order that nothing may ever separate us or disunite us from You, but that we may be always faithful and constant in this resolution. We sacrifice to the love of Your Sacred Heart all that can give vain pleasure to our hearts and all that can engross them uselessly with the things of this world where we confess that everything besides loving and serving You alone is vanity and affliction of spirit. O Divine and most amiable Lord and Saviour Jesus Christ, may You be blessed, loved and glorified eternally. Amen.

Act of Reparation to the Sacred Heart of Jesus

O Divine Heart of Jesus, inexhaustible Source of love and goodness, ah! How I regret that I have forgotten You so much and loved You so little. O Sacred Heart, You merit the reverence and love of all hearts which You have cherished so much and laid under infinite obligations. And yet You receive from the greater number nothing but ingratitude and coldness, and especially from my own heart which merits Your just indignation. But Your Heart is all full of goodness and mercy, and of this I wish to avail myself to obtain reconciliation and pardon. O Divine Heart, I grieve intensely when I see myself guilty of such cowardice and when I consider the ungrateful conduct of my wicked heart, which has so unjustly stolen the love that it owes to You and bestowed it on myself or on vain amusements.

O Heart most meek, if the sorrow and shame of a heart that recognizes its error can satisfy You, pardon this heart of mine for it is sorry for its infidelity and ashamed of the little care which it has taken to please You by its love. O Sacred Heart of my Saviour, what could I expect from all this but Your displeasure and condign punishment if I did not hope in Your mercy. O, Heart of my God, Heart most holy, Heart to which alone belongs to pardon sinners, do You in Your mercy pardon this poor miserable heart of mine.

All its powers unite in a supreme effort to make reparation to You for its wanderings from You and the disordered application of its love.

Ah! How have I been able to refuse You my heart, I who have so many obligations to make You its sole possessor, nevertheless I have done so. But now how I regret that I have wandered away from You, from the love of You who are the Source of all goodness, in a word, from the Heart of my Jesus, who although needing me not, has sought me out and lavished Your favours on me. O adorable Heart of Jesus, is it possible that my heart can have treated You thus, my heart which depends entirely on Your love and Your benefits and which, if You should take them from it, would fall into the utmost extremes of misery or be reduced to nothingness? Ah! How I am beholden to Your goodness, O indulgent Heart of my Saviour, for having borne with me so long in my ingratitude! Oh! How timely Your mercies come to pardon my poor, inconstant heart!

O Heart of my Jesus, I now consecrate to You and give You all my love and the source of my love, which is my heart; I give You both irrevocably, although with great confusion for having so long refused You your own possessions. O Divine Heart, my very capability of bestowing my poor heart on You is a proof of Your great love for me, but alas! I have availed myself badly of such a favourable opportunity to merit Your love and grace. Oh! How great is my confusion at the thought of this! O Heart of my Jesus, reform my faithless heart, grant that, going forward, it may bind itself to Your love by its own, and that it may approach You as much in the future as it has wandered away from You in the past, and as You are the Creator of my heart, may You, I beg You, one day give it the crown of immortality.

Litany of the Sacred Heart of Jesus

Lord, have mercy on us.
Christ, have mercy on us.
Lord, have mercy on us.
Christ, hear us.

Christ, graciously hear us.

God the Father of heaven,

God the Son, Redeemer of the world,

God the Holy Ghost,

Holy Trinity, one God,

Heart of Jesus,

Heart of Jesus, formed in the womb of a virgin mother,

Heart of Jesus united to the Word of God,

Heart of Jesus, sanctuary of the Divinity,

Heart of Jesus, temple of the Holy Trinity,

Heart of Jesus, temple of holiness,

Heart of Jesus, fountain of all graces,

Heart of Jesus, full of sweetness and humility,

Heart of Jesus, furnace of love,

Heart of Jesus, source of contrition,

Heart of Jesus, treasure of wisdom,

Heart of Jesus, ocean of goodness,

Heart of Jesus, throne of mercy,

Heart of Jesus, model of all virtues,

Heart of Jesus, house of God and gate of heaven,

Heart of Jesus, inexhaustible treasure,

Heart of Jesus, of whose fulness we have all received,

Heart of Jesus full of mercy to those who invoke You,

Heart of Jesus, our peace and our atonement,

Heart of Jesus, living sacrifice, holy and agreeable to God,

Heart of Jesus, atoning for our sins,

Heart of Jesus, fountain of water, springing up into everlasting life,

Heart of Jesus, spring of living water,

Heart of Jesus, sorrowful in the garden, even unto death,

Heart of Jesus, weakened by a sweat of blood,

Heart of Jesus, humiliated for our sake,

Heart of Jesus, filled with sorrow for our sins,

Heart of Jesus, made obedient, even to the death of the cross,

Heart of Jesus, pierced by a spear,

Heart of Jesus, exhausted of Your blood on the cross,

Heart of Jesus, refuge of sinners,

Heart of Jesus, strength of the just,

Heart of Jesus, consolation of the afflicted,

Heart of Jesus, support of those who are tempted,

Heart of Jesus, terror of the evil spirits,

Heart of Jesus, perseverance of the just,

Heart of Jesus, hope of the dying,

Heart of Jesus, joy of the saints,

Heart of Jesus, king and centre of all hearts,

From all sin, Lord Jesus, deliver us.

From hardness of heart, Lord Jesus, deliver us.

From everlasting death, Lord Jesus, deliver us.

Lamb of God, who takest away the sins of the world: spare us, O Jesus.

Lamb of God, who takest away the sins of the world: graciously hear us, O Jesus.

Lamb of God, who takest away the sins of the world: graciously hear us, O Jesus.

Lamb of God who takest away the sins of the world: have mercy on us, O Jesus.

Jesus, hear us.

Jesus, graciously hear us.

First Saturday Devotion

Meditation and Prayers in the company of the Blessed Virgin Mary: opening prayers

Almighty and everlasting God, Creator of Heaven and Earth, You created us in holiness and love for Yourself only. We, the people of God, have assembled here under the banner and patronage of Our

Lady of Fatima to meditate with her the message which, in your merciful love, you willed that the Virgin Mother of Your Son should carry to her children on earth.

Almighty God, we remember that in the days of old, You sent Your holy prophets to warn the rebellious children of Israel whenever they strayed from Your ways. These Your holy prophets gave warnings of the consequences of sin and through punishment and penance You brought them to holiness. In our day, You have sent us the Blessed Virgin Mary, the new Eve promised of old to remind us of the dangers and darkness facing the world. She carried us this message from our true God to open our eyes to our miserable spiritual condition that we have brought on ourselves through disobedience of God's commandments and our determination to instal in our midst strongholds of spiritual and moral perversions which seek to replace God's truth. Our Holy Mother mercifully reminds us that in our pursuit of temporal affairs, we have neglected our true end which is God our Creator. She calls us to arm ourselves with the sure weapons against evil: prayer, penance, sacrifice and faithful observance of the sacraments, especially the Eucharist.

Oh Father of us all, bless this assembly of your people, deliver us from spiritual darkness and eternal death. May we come to know You by the faithful observance of Your commandments which is the surest way to peace in our families, communities and the world. On our part, we promise to start the process of true repentance, reparation for our sins and those of the whole world.

Meditation on the First Apparition of the Angel

Let us read Lucia's account of the children's first encounter with the angel:

"After having taken our lunch and said our prayers, we began to see, some distance off, above the trees that stretched away towards the east, a light, whiter than snow, in the form of a young man, transparent, and brighter than crystal pierced by the rays of the sun. As he drew nearer, we could distinguish his features more and more clearly. We were surprised, absorbed, and struck dumb with amazement."

Lucia goes on to describe how the angel knelt on the ground and bowed down until his head touched the ground and recited the following prayer: "My God, I believe, I adore, I hope and love You! I ask pardon of You for those who do not believe, do not adore, do not hope, and do not love You!"

Let us all repeat the words of the angel three times.

The angel finally implored the children to pray because the hearts of Jesus and Mary were attentive to their prayers. Let us all pray with sincere hearts deeply meditating on the hearts of Jesus and Mary which have loved us so much. (The First Mystery of the rosary)

The Second Apparition of the Angel

In the second apparition, the angel spoke as follows: "Pray! Pray very much. The Hearts of Jesus and Mary have designs of mercy on you. Offer prayers and sacrifices constantly to the most high." He explained further: "Make of everything you can a sacrifice, and offer it to God as an act of reparation for the sins by which He is offended, and in supplication for the conversion of sinners. You will thus draw down peace upon your country. I am its guardian angel, the Angel of Portugal. Above all, accept and bear with submission, the suffering which the Lord will send you." (Second decade of the rosary)

Prayer

God our Father, bless us that we may seriously reflect on your mysteries and especially to understand the value of prayers and sacrifices for our salvation and enlighten our minds so that we may know You through the observance of Your commandments. Also, through observing Your commandments, we may find joy in Your presence and love You with sincere heart. It is only by truly loving You that we can be Your true children in Christ and help in the redemption of our fellow human beings.

The Third Apparition of the Angel: meditation on the story of Lucia

Lucia described how the angel appeared holding a chalice in his hands with a host above it and that drops of blood were falling into the chalice. She said the angel left the chalice and the host suspended in the air, prostrated on the ground and said the following prayer three times:

"Most Holy Trinity, Father, Son and Holy Spirit, I adore You profoundly, and I offer You the most precious Body, Blood, Soul and Divinity of Jesus Christ, present in all the tabernacles of the world, in reparation for the outrages, sacrileges and indifference with which He Himself is offended. And through the infinite merits of His most Sacred Heart, and the Immaculate Heart of Mary, I beg of You the conversion of poor sinners." (Repeat three times)

Lucia concluded by revealing that the angel gave the Blood of Christ in the chalice to Francisco and Jacinta but gave her only the consecrated Host, saying the following prayer:

"Take and drink the Body and Blood of Jesus Christ, horribly outraged by ungrateful men. Repair their crimes and console your God." (A decade of the rosary)

Meditation on the Appearance of the Angel of Portugal

The role that the angel fulfilled at Fatima is not different from the part that angels have played in the sacred scripture. They were created to serve God's purposes, to adore Him and serve Him as faithful messengers and protect mankind against the forces of Satan. When Moses was crossing the desert as leader of the Israelites, God told him: "Behold, I send an angel before you, to guard you on the way and to bring you to the place which I have prepared. Give heed to him and hearken to his voice. Do not rebel against him, for he will not pardon your transgression; for my name is in him." (Exod. 23, 20-21). Also in Psalm 91, the following is stated: "Because you have made the Lord your refuge, the most high your habitation, no evil shall befall you, no scourge come near your tent. For He will give his angels charge of you to guard you in all your ways. On their hands, they will bear you up, lest you dash your foot against the stone." It is therefore not surprising that the presence of the angel had the following effect on Lucia: "The force of the presence of God was so intense that it absolved us and almost completely annihilated us." The angel therefore came to prepare the children for the arrival of the Mother of God by recalling to their minds the need for faith, love of God and the truth of our redemption through the Eucharist.

Messages of the Blessed Virgin Mary to the World from the apparitions of Fatima

First Apparition on 13th May 1917

1   Our Lady confirmed to the children that she came from heaven. To confirm this, she disclosed to the children the whereabouts of their two friends who had died: One was in purgatory and the other was in heaven.

2   Our Lady disclosed that because God wanted to use them for His purposes, they would undergo sufferings and trials but that they must accept the trials as reparation for the conversion of sinners. She assured them however that God would send them graces to strengthen them in all their trials.

3   Our Lady blessed the children, sending them graces that penetrated their souls and, according to Lucia, it helped them to see themselves in God who was light making them fall on their knees, repeating in their hearts the following prayer: "Oh Most Holy Trinity, I adore You! My God, My God, I love You in the most Blessed Sacrament."

Second Apparition on 13th June 1917

1   Our Lady revealed to the children the importance of praying the rosary.

2   She entrusted to Lucia a mission that she would live long to spread the message and devotion of Fatima and like the true

163

prophet of God, predicted the early death of the other two children Jacinta and Francisco.

3   The children could see in the palm of Our Lady's right hand, a heart encircled by thorns which pierced it. The children were made to understand that it was the Immaculate Heart of Mary outraged by the sins of humanity and seeking reparation.

Third Apparition on 13th July 1917

1   Our Lady repeated the importance of saying the rosary for peace in the world because only she could intercede to end wars and conflicts.

2   She repeated the need for sacrifice on behalf of sinners and the saying of the following prayer whenever we make some sacrifice: "Jesus, it is for love of You, for the conversion of sinners and in reparation for the sins committed against the Immaculate Heart of Mary."

3   Our Lady opened her hands and rays of light penetrated the earth making the children have a vision of hell which came as a sea of fire. They saw the fire of hell, demons and souls in human form. Our Lady told the children "You have seen hell where the souls of poor sinners go. To save them, God wishes to establish in the world devotion to my Immaculate Heart. If what I say to you is done, many souls will be saved and there will be peace in the world."

4   Our Lady requested the children that they should say after each mystery of the rosary the following prayer: "Oh my Jesus, forgive us, save us from the fire of hell. Lead all souls to heaven, especially those who are most in need."

Fourth and Fifth Apparition on 13th August 1917

1   She repeated the need for prayers and sacrifices for sinners because many souls go to hell, as there are no people sacrificing themselves and praying for them.

Sixth Apparition on 13th September 1917

1   She repeated the need to pray the rosary for peace in the world and like God's prophet, disclosed that she would appear the following month with Saint Joseph and the Child Jesus to bless the world and that God was pleased with the sacrifices of the children.

Seventh Apparition on 13th October 1917

1   The prophecy was fulfilled when Saint Joseph appeared with the Child Jesus and Our Lady, robed in white with a blue mantle. Saint Joseph and the Child Jesus blessed the world, tracing the sign of the cross with their hands.

2   Our Lord also appeared with Our Lady as Our Lady of Dolours and Our Lord blessed the world.

3   Our Lady appeared alone as Our Lady of Mount Carmel holding the scapular.

Special Message to Lucia on 10th December 1925

Our Lady appeared to Lucia with the Child Jesus and said the following: "Have compassion on the Heart of Your Most Holy Mother, covered with thorns with which men pierce it at every moment, and there is no one to make an act of reparation to remove them." She was referring to people's blasphemies against her and ingratitude.

She promised to assist at the hour of death, with the graces necessary for salvation, all those who, on the first Saturday of five consecutive months shall confess, receive Holy Communion and recite five decades of the rosary with the intention of making reparations to her.

On the question of this first Saturday devotion, Lucia had an encounter with the Child Jesus on the 15th February 1926, during which Our Lord made revelations on the making of the first Saturday devotion. Our Lord requested that in order to receive the full graces that are promised by that devotion, it would please Him more if the devotions were done with fervour and with the intention of making reparation to the Immaculate Heart of Mary and not with the sole purpose of obtaining the benefits of salvation.

Act of Consecration to the Immaculate Heart of Mary

O Immaculate Heart of Mary, Queen of Heaven and Earth and tender Mother of men, in accordance with thy ardent wish made known at Fatima, I consecrate to thee myself, my brethren, my country and the whole human race. Reign over us and teach us how to make the Heart of Jesus reign and triumph in us as it has reigned and triumphed in thee.

Reign over us, dearest Mother, that we may be Thine in prosperity and in adversity; in joy and in sorrow; in health and in sickness; in life and in death. O most compassionate Heart of Mary, Queen of Virgins, watch over our minds and our hearts and preserve them from the deluge of impurity which Thou didst lament so sorrowfully at Fatima. We want to be pure like Thee. We want to atone for the many sins committed against Jesus and Thee. We want to call down upon our country and the whole world the peace of God in justice and charity.

Therefore, we now promise to imitate Thy virtues by the practice of a Christian life without regard to human respect. We resolve to receive Holy Communion on the First Saturday of every month and to offer Thee five decades of the Rosary each day together with our sacrifices in a spirit of reparation and penance. Amen.

Act of Reparation to the Immaculate Heart of Mary

Most Holy Virgin, and Our beloved Mother, we listen with grief to the complaints of Thy Immaculate Heart, surrounded with thorns which ungrateful men place therein at every moment by their blasphemies and ingratitude. Moved by the ardent desire of loving Thee as our Mother and of promoting true devotion to the Immaculate Heart, we prostrate ourselves at Thy feet to prove the sorrow we feel for the grief that men cause Thee and to atone by means of our prayers and sacrifices for the offenses with which men return Thy tender love. Obtain for them and for us the pardon of so many sins. A word from Thee will obtain grace and forgiveness for us all. Hasten O Lady, the conversion of sinners, that they may love Jesus and cease to offend God, already so much offended, and thus avoid eternal punishment. Turn Thine eyes of mercy toward us so that henceforth we may love God with all our hearts while on Earth and enjoy Him forever in Heaven. Amen.

Devotion to Saint Joseph

Reason for Devotion

The eternal Father, in appointing Saint Joseph as Head of the Holy Family and to be the guardian of Jesus and Mary wished to place all mankind under his protection: St Joseph should therefore be venerated for the singular responsibility entrusted to him by God the Father who entrusted him with the saviour of the world and the incarnate word.

Jesus acknowledged and honoured Saint Joseph as the representative of the Eternal Father and treated him as a Father. Since our Blessed Saviour was a perfect Man for our imitation, Saint Joseph could only be a perfect Father. "He was subject to them."

A creator and God, through His incomprehensible glory and dignity could only subject Himself to a sublimely elevated Father.

Our Lady to Saint Bridget. "So obedient was my Son, that if Joseph said to Him, Do this or that, He instantly did it."

God in His plan of salvation, uses the Holy Family to affirm the human family and the commandments to honour parents. Therefore the Church also as a family honours a special human father, Joseph. Indeed, Jesus recommended to Saint Margaret of Corlona to be especially devoted to Saint Joseph for the sake of the gratitude which He felt towards him, for having provided for His earthly wants with so much zeal and affection.

Virgin Mary

Saint Albert the Great describes Saint Joseph as the protector and patron of Mary: as the defender of her honour and virginity (purity). Mary confirmed her honour for Saint Joseph in two apparitions.

Saint Teresa of Avila

Our Lady revealed to Saint Teresa her gratitude for the honour which the saint had given Saint Joseph by spreading devotion to him throughout the Church.

Saint Gertrude

Our Lady opened the gates of Heaven and revealed the incomparable brilliance of the throne which Saint Joseph occupied and how the saints in Heaven honoured him. Both human and Church families honour Jesus, Mary and Joseph.

Exceptional Status of Saint Joseph

Exceptional purity and virginity: exceptional because God created that circumstance for our redemption while conferring on him the fatherhood of the Holy Family. The Union of the Unified Hearts of Jesus and Mary constituted the merit and glory of Mary and Joseph. In the Church's teaching, therefore, after the Holy Trinity, Mary is the most exalted human creature followed by Joseph.

Happy Death: Saint Joseph

Saint Joseph is acknowledged by the Church to be the special advocate of dying Christians. As the foster father of Jesus, he is formidable to the devil. Since he himself died in the presence of Jesus and Mary, he died a model human death, that is in the embrace of Jesus.

Specific Graces and Favours

Venerable Sister Zaguoni, a Franciscan nun who had been especially devoted to Saint Joseph, saw Saint Joseph holding the Child Jesus in his arms. The religious present actually heard her conversing with the Child Jesus.

In another instance, a capuchin, devoted to Saint Joseph, dying on the 19th March, the Feast of Saint Joseph, cried out "Behold the Queen of Heaven! Behold Saint Joseph." and then died immediately.

Saint Vincent Ferrer relates how Jesus, Mary and Joseph came to visit a dying merchant in Valencia, Spain. This merchant was in the habit of inviting one old man, one woman and a child every Christmas, in honour of the Holy Family. He especially honoured these poor invitees, revering them, through faith, as he would the Holy Family. After his death he appeared to some people who were praying for his departed soul and revealed to them that, just before his death, he saw Jesus, Mary and Joseph who told him that they had come to take him to paradise because of the way he had honoured them while on earth.

A nun, Sister Anne of Saint Augustine was visited just before her death by Saint Joseph, Saint Teresa of Avila and a multitude of saints. Just at the same time, a Carmelite in another monastery who was praying for the sick nun saw her ascending to heaven accompanied by Saint Joseph and Saint Teresa with a following of angels and saints.

Novena to Saint Joseph

First Day

Oh Blessed Joseph, True and Worthy Spouse of Our Blessed Mother. You were destined from all eternity to be the Spouse of the Mother of God. In this most worthy vocation, you had a special honour of being chosen by the adorable Trinity. By special divine light, you were able to perform the impossible vocation of making your home in Nazareth, a place of reconciliation between God and man, between Heaven and earth. You were therefore raised to a dignity which no other preacher, either man or angel was deemed worthy to share. I, an unworthy servant of God, therefore beg you to obtain for me, the grace to imitate your great love of purity, the strength to overcome all trials and temptations and to obtain the virtues to which your co-operation with divine grace raised you in this world.

Second Day

Oh Blessed Joseph, you were chosen by God your heavenly Father, to represent Him as Father of His Son on earth. You were given the extra-ordinary honour to exercise parental authority over Our Lord Jesus Christ. Jesus Himself was pleased to be obedient to you and, was ready to undertake all labours to help you to provide for His wants and to protect Him from danger. For the sake of the humility with which you performed this exalted position, obtain for me a strong and tender love for Jesus, especially love for Him in the Holy Eucharist so that I may become one with Him as He and the Father are one. Be a Father to me too and may divine love transform me, through your intercession into a little child in your arms.

Third Day

Oh Father Joseph, how glorious was your dignity as the Father of Jesus Christ. You were made the master of the Saviour and were given the power to do with him as a Father would do to a child. Jesus became a sharer in all your labours and hardships, thank you for your profound respect for the adorable person of Jesus Christ and the humility with which you exercised authority over him. Through your perfect example, teach all your children how to exercise authority. May we consider all authority as given to us by God and may we exercise it according to God's will and holding all offices in place of God, we may treat our brothers and sisters with true charity, respect and kindness.

Fourth Day

Oh Holy Joseph, the Holy Spirit gave you the title of "Just", which meant that you possessed exemplary virtues. Your holiness made you worthy to be the spouse of the Mother of God and to be the foster father of His son. By the purity of your heart, you became detached from all worldly things and through obedience to God's will, you advanced in perfection. We honour and revere your extra-ordinary holiness which places you above all other saints. Obtain for me, Oh my dear Father and patron, the grace to worthily receive the Eucharist so that like Christ, I may show God's charity to mankind.

Fifth Day

Saint Joseph, you were a model of justice in your duties to God. Your only desire was to obey God's will perfectly. You were also a model of justice towards your neighbour, in thought, word and action.

Faced with the incomprehensible mystery of the incarnation, you nevertheless showed perfect charity towards a Blessed Virgin Mary and never complained in helping to fulfil God's plan of salvation. You indeed became our divine Lord's first disciple. Teach us therefore the way to observe God's law with perfect humility and always to seek the inspiration of the Holy Spirit, to love our neighbour and to serve God in our neighbour to the utmost of our ability.

Sixth Day

Saint Joseph, you were the crown of all the patriarchs and all the ancestors of the promised Messiah. All their virtues were concentrated and perfected in your person. You were also the crown of the saints of the New Testament because as the head of the Holy Family, of which Jesus Christ was a member, you proved yourself most worthy and so surpassed all the other saints of God in glory. Pray for us therefore to imitate your lively and most fruitful works and your zeal for the honour of God and salvation of man. Elevated as you now are in heaven, forget not your poor miserable children on Earth so that one day, we shall taste of the fruits of glory with you in heaven.

Seventh Day

Oh Saint Joseph, you were especially favoured, assisted and honoured by the angels. From them you received comfort in your anguish and light and direction in times of difficulties. With their help, you were able to discharge your duty as the guardian angel of Jesus and Mary. You discharged these functions with your virtues of simplicity, innocence and fervour. We turn to you then, with an ardent desire to conform ourselves perfectly to the Divine Infant whom you protected. Obtain for us all the virtues we need for Christian living. May we be guided by the assistance of the angels and saints of God.

Eighth Day

Saint Joseph, you were the model of all those who engaged in interior recollection and through silence, retirement and prayer, are led to contemplate God's gifts to mankind and show greater love of God.

But you were also a model of the active life by your care of the Holy Family. You were therefore ready to assist your neighbour in the law of God as and when necessary. Pray for us to learn recollection and care while avoiding all useless conversation and the cares of this world. May we imitate your virtues and learn to converse with God and be prepared to glorify him eternally with you after this life.

Ninth Day

Oh Blessed Saint Joseph, even in this life you found happiness because you saw Man-God face to face for thirty years as the foster father of Jesus. You also beheld the Holy Life and charity of Jesus Christ and imitated them perfectly. Through your intercession, help us to overcome our passions for earthly things and rather devote our minds and hearts to the contemplation of things which are spiritual and heavenly. Pray for us for a strong and lively faith, in order to become detached from all earthly things. By contemplating Jesus Christ in the Eucharist, may we do good works so that even in this life of sorrow, we may have a foretaste of the happiness which awaits us in heaven.

Litany of Saint Joseph

Lord, have mercy on us.

Christ, have mercy on us.

Lord, have mercy on us.

Christ, hear us.

Christ, graciously hear us.

God, the Father of heaven, have mercy on us.

God the Son, Redeemer of the world, have mercy on us.

God the Holy Ghost, have mercy on us.

Holy Trinity, one God, have mercy on us.

Holy Mary, spouse of Saint Joseph,

Saint Joseph, spouse of Mary, the mother of Jesus,

St Joseph, virgin spouse of a virgin mother,

Saint Joseph, guardian of the virginity of Mary,

Saint Joseph, father of the Son of God,

Saint Joseph, nurse of the Child Jesus,
Saint Joseph, organ of the Word reduced to silence,
Saint Joseph, redeemer of our Redeemer,
Saint Joseph, saviour of our Saviour,
Saint Joseph, guide of Jesus in His flight,
Saint Joseph, teacher of incarnate Wisdom,
Saint Joseph, minister of the great council,
Saint Joseph, depository of the celestial treasure,
Saint Joseph, man of consummate justice,
Saint Joseph, model of perfect obedience,
Saint Joseph, lily of spotless purity,
Saint Joseph, zealous lover of our souls,
Saint Joseph, protector of religious houses,
Saint Joseph, defender of the agonizing,
Saint Joseph, patron of those who die in the Lord,
Lamb of God, who takes away the sins of the world,
spare us, O Lord.
Lamb of God, who takes away the sins of the world,
hear us, O Lord.
Lamb of God, who takes away the sins of the world,
have mercy on us.
Pray for us, O Holy Saint Joseph.
That we may be made worthy of the promises of
Christ.

Let Us Pray

Be mindful of us, o Blessed Joseph! And grant us the assistance
of your protection with Him who has called you father; and also
render favourable to us the most Blessed Virgin, your spouse, and the
mother of Him, who, with the Father and the Holy Ghost, lives and
reigns for ever and ever. Amen.

Prayers in Honour of the Seven Dolours and Joys of St Joseph

Chaste spouse of the Immaculate Mother of Jesus! Glorious
St. Joseph! permit me to commemorate the mental agony which

you endured with regard to your sacred spouse; deeming yourself under the painful necessity of leaving her, until the angel banished your doubts, and filled you with unspeakable joy, by revealing the mystery of the Incarnation: by your anguish and holy joy on this occasion, obtain for me, I implore, both now and in my agony, the joy of a good conscience, sincere charity towards all men, and the consolation of dying with you in the embraces of Jesus and Mary.

Our Father, Hail Mary, Gloria

O thrice happy Joseph! Deeply impressed with a sense of the sweet and sacred duties which, as a father, you were called on to render to the "Word Incarnate", permit me to commemorate the sorrow which filled your breast on beholding that Divine Infant lying on straw, in a manger, weeping, shivering with cold, and enduring all the privations of the most abject poverty. But how great was your consolation shortly after, to hear the canticle of peace intoned by the blessed spirits, and to witness the kings of the earth humbly prostrate at the Infant's feet, while their countenances beamed with love, joy and admiration, and offering their most precious gifts to Him whom they acknowledged as heaven's King! By your anguish and holy joy on this occasion, obtain that my heart may be always a pure and holy sanctuary, where Jesus will love to dwell by His grace and His real presence in the adorable Eucharist; and that, when the trials of life and the shades of death shall have passed away, my ears may be enchanted with the harmonies of the heavenly choirs, and that I may enter into the possession of those joys that neither eye has seen, ear heard, nor the human heart conceived. Amen.

Our Father, Hail Mary, Gloria.

You were, O great Saint Joseph! a man according to God's own heart, for His Law was your meditation. Permit me to commemorate the acute sensibility of your tender heart, when by the law of circumcision, it became your painful duty to cause the first effusion of the precious blood of the innocent "Lamb". The sword which pierced His Infant flesh wounded your heart; but the sweet name of "Jesus", which, in accordance with the revelation of the angel, you did bestow on Him, imparted a holy and soothing unction to your soul. By your anguish and holy joy on this occasion, pray that your Blessed Son, that, being purified in the laver of His precious blood, and all inordinate inclinations being circumcised, I may have the sweet and saving name of "Jesus" always engraven on my heart, and be so happy as to invoke it with great love and efficacy at the hour of death. Amen.

Our Father, Hail Mary, Gloria.

O Faithful Saint Joseph! to whom the mysterious secrets of our redemption were confided, permit me to commemorate the sorrow which filled your afflicted ear on hearing Simeon's prophecy concerning the sufferings of Jesus and Mary. But how much were you comforted on hearing immediately after that the Child Jesus was destined for the resurrection and salvation of many! By your anguish and holy joy on this occasion, obtain for me grace to participate in the dolours of Mary, and the bitter passion of her beloved Son, that by patient suffering, and heartfelt compunction, I may one day rise to a glorious resurrection, through the merits of Jesus Christ, and the intercession of His most Blessed Mother. Amen.

Our Father, Hail Mary, Gloria.

O Zealous guardian of the Son of God, and pious comforter of His dear mother! permit me to commemorate the trials and anxiety you underwent in their service, but especially in your flight into Egypt, and the hardships of your exile, for which, however, you were in some degree consoled, by seeing the idols fall prostrate in the presence of the only true God. By your sufferings and holy joy on this occasion, obtain for me, I beg of you, grace to destroy all the idols of self-love to which I may have erected an altar in my heart, and that, henceforth, devoting all the energies of my soul to the service of you and Mary, I may live and die as you did in union with them. Amen.

Our Father, Hail Mary, Gloria.

Angel of the Earth! Vigilant guardian of the Virgin of virgins and her Blessed babe! Permit me to commemorate your painful anxiety for their safety, when, on returning home, you found the throne occupied by a tyrant no less cruel than Herod; but soon, reassured by an angel, you joyfully re-established your family in the holy house of Nazareth. By your anguish and holy joy on this occasion, obtain for me, I most earnestly implore, the great blessings of interior peace, and a pure conscience during life, and that I may die invoking the sweet names of Jesus and Mary. Amen.

Mirror of sanctity! Glorious Saint Joseph! Permit me to commemorate the affliction which you experienced on losing the Child Jesus, and the agony of your grief upon finding your search useless after the space of three days. But how inexpressible was your joy upon finding your precious treasure in the house of prayer! By your poignant anguish and ineffable joy on this occasion, obtain for me grace never to be separated from Jesus by grievous sin. And should I have the misfortune to forfeit His friendship, even partially, by venial sin, may I never suffer the day to close until I shall have made my peace with God; but especially at the hour of death, may I be closely united to Him by love, confidence, and perfect compunction. Amen.

Our Father, Hail Mary, Gloria.

Pray for us, O Holy Saint Joseph!
That we may be made worthy of the promises of Christ.

Let Us Pray

Grant, O Lord! that we may be helped by the merits of Your most holy mother's spouse; and that what of ourselves we cannot obtain, may be given us through his intercession; who lives and reigns, world without end. Amen.

Chaplet of Saint Michael

Saint Michael appearing one day to Antonia d'Astonac, a most devout Servant of God, told her that he wished to be honoured by nine salutations corresponding to the nine choirs of angels, which should consist of one Our Father and three Hail Marys in honour of each of the angelic choirs.

Promises of Saint Michael

Whosoever would practise this devotion in his honour would have, when approaching the Holy Table, an escort of nine angels chosen from each one of the nine choirs. In addition, for the daily recital of these nine salutations he promised his continual assistance and that of all the holy angels during life, and after death deliverance from purgatory for themselves and their relations.

Method of Reciting the Chaplet

The Chaplet is begun by saying the following invocation on the medal:

> O God, come to my assistance.
> O Lord, make haste to help me.
> Glory be to the Father, etc.
> Say one Our Father and three Hail Marys after each of the following nine salutations in honour of the nine choirs of angels.
> By the intercession of Saint Michael and the celestial choir of seraphim, may the Lord make us worthy to burn with the fire of perfect charity. Amen.
> By the intercession of Saint Michael and the celestial

choir of cherubim, may the Lord vouchsafe to grant us grace to leave the ways of wickedness to run in the paths of Christian perfection. Amen.

By the intercession of Saint Michael and the celestial choir of thrones, may the Lord infuse into our hearts a true and sincere spirit of humility. Amen.

By the intercession of Saint Michael and the celestial choir of dominion, may the Lord give us grace to govern our senses and subdue our unruly passions. Amen.

By the intercession of Saint Michael and the celestial choir of powers, may the Lord vouchsafe to protect our souls against the snare and temptations of the Devil. Amen.

By the intercession of Saint Michael and the celestial choir of virtues may the Lord preserve us from evil and suffer us not to fall into temptation. Amen.

By the intercession of Saint Michael and the celestial choir of principalities, may God fill our souls with a true spirit of obedience. Amen.

By the intercession of Saint Michael and the celestial choir of archangels, may the Lord give us perseverance in faith and in all good works, in order that we gain the glory of paradise. Amen.

By the intercession of Saint Michael and the celestial choir of angels, may the Lord grant us to be protected by them in this mortal life and conducted hereafter to eternal glory. Amen.

Say one Our Father in honour of each of the following leading angels:

Saint Michael, Saint Gabriel, Saint Raphael, our guardian angel.

The Chaplet is concluded with the following prayers: O Glorious Prince, Saint Michael, chief and commander of the heavenly hosts, guardian of souls, vanquisher of rebel spirits, servant in the house of the Divine King, and our admirable conductor, you who shine with excellence and superhuman virtue, vouchsafe to deliver us from all evil, who turn to you with confidence, and enable us by your gracious protection to serve God more and more faithfully every day.

Pray for us, O glorious Saint Michael, Prince of the Church of Jesus Christ.

That we may be made worthy of His Promises.

Almighty and Everlasting God, who by a prodigy of goodness and a merciful desire of the salvation of all people, have appointed the most glorious Archangel Saint Michael, Prince of Your Church, make us worthy, we beg You to be delivered from all our enemies that none of them may harass us at the hour of death, but that we may be conducted by him into the august presence of Your Divine Majesty. This we beg through the merits of Jesus Christ our Lord. Amen.

Conclusion

Through His mysterious encounter with Saint Faustina, Christ comes to renew the scriptural message of Divine Mercy. But He has also come to proclaim God's favour because He told Saint Faustina that He has come not as a judge but to distribute mercy to specified souls who are in a state of despair. It was His will that all these souls, according to their circumstances, should turn to God's mercy.

We see in the novena that the groups of persons Our Lord wished to be prayed for are sinners, priests and religious, devout and faithful souls, pagans, heretics, children and /or humble souls, devotees to Divine Mercy, souls in purgatory and lukewarm souls. In His divinity, Christ saw that all these souls could be in despair and therefore needed to turn to God's mercy. He, as the Redeemer of mankind, made sacrifices for these souls but He revealed to Saint Faustina that they could only reach their heavenly destination if they always turn to His mercy.

We further learn from Christ's encounter with Saint Faustina that in order to gain redemption for ourselves and our neighbour, we must respond to God's call by living according to the Spirit and thereby overcome the flesh. In this we imitate Christ Himself who proclaimed in the temple that the Spirit of God was upon Him before He could proclaim the Good News. So, to accomplish God's purposes, we must join ourselves to Christ so that, in the measure permitted by God, we can do great things for God and for our fellow humans.

By accepting that we must live by Spirit, we allow God's gifts to flow into us. The Father bestows the gifts by sending the Spirit through the merits of His Son, Our Lord Jesus Christ. This life in the Spirit ensures that we gain the knowledge and strength necessary for our earthly life.

What Does Life in the Spirit Bring?

St Paul, in his letter to the Galatians, speaks as follows on the importance of living according to the Spirit: "Let me say this; learn to live and move in the Spirit; then there is no danger of your giving way to the impulses of corrupt nature. The impulses of nature and the impulses of the Spirit are at war with one another; either is clean contrary to the other, and that is why you cannot do all that your will approves. It is by letting the Spirit lead you that you free yourself from the yoke of the law."

So it is by being led by the Spirit that we can fruitfully lead our new life of grace in Jesus Christ. We are able to accept our new role as His disciples and take up our crosses to follow Him. We then become partners in His saving love and work of redemption by imitating His earthly sacrifices. By imitating Him, all His merits and virtues are manifested in us.

Let the experience of the Prodigal Son help us, in this matter of living by the Spirit. The poor child of a wealthy person, who found himself in misery working to feed herds of swine, suddenly came to his senses. "Why am I ruining my life? I am of greater value than this. I am entitled to servants and decent existence." He renounced his life of misery and returned to his merciful father.

By not living by the Spirit, we live in misery because we have failed to meditate on our true value. It is only by living in the Spirit of Christ that we are constantly reminded of our true value. Through new spiritual insights, we see ourselves participating in God's glory. What this means can only be appreciated through living by the Spirit in Christ. Christ makes us appreciate what grace has done to our visible human nature. We are able to thank Him now, not only for what He has accomplished for us, but especially for the price of our redemption. It is then that, out of gratitude, we are prepared to renounce our pride, pleasures, ambitions, selfishness and other earthly passions in order to accomplish God's purposes.

To encourage us to live by the Spirit, Christ conveys the critical message, through Saint Faustina, that we should trust in His mercy.

Trust is self-surrender to the riches of God's mercy, a spiritual posture that allows God to accomplish His designs of mercy in us. It is an acceptance of his infinite and unfathomable wisdom. It is from this wisdom that He sent Christ, His only begotten Son, to empty Himself of His heavenly glory in order to redeem us from our spiritual enemies.

St Ephraem makes an interesting observation on the question of trust, and the depth of God's wisdom. "He who comes into contact with some share of its treasure should not think that the only thing contained in the word is what he himself has found. He should realize that he has only been able to find that one thing from among many others."

Our trust in God, as we have already said, is not blind. The Father of all mercies has manifested His ways to humanity over the ages. He has manifested His power and faithfulness and has vowed that all His promises will be fulfilled. As our Creator who knows all things, He knows that redemption is available to all who will it and that His judgement will be just. He is a merciful God.

The devotions and messages in this book should be a spiritual companion for Christians and non-Christians alike. Christ has proclaimed favour for all humanity. The Special Retreat should provide a special help for all who seek to meditate on His work of redemption. Through the devotions, we can be assured of a continuous life in the Spirit and great spiritual strength to overcome our rebellious nature as well as our spiritual enemies.

But, in all things, Christ must constantly be on our minds. It is through Him that all things were created and it is He who comes to redeem His own. It is Christ who, until the fulness of time, stands before the throne of His Father in heaven bringing graces for our redemption through His Sacred Heart.

Through Saint Faustina, the first saint of the 21st century, Christ comes to manifest once again the truths of our salvation but this time to emphasise that, in place of human despair, He has brought great mercies.

Summary of the Devotions

Novena to the Divine Mercy

Christ to Saint Faustina: "I desire that during these nine days you bring souls to the fountain of My mercy, that they may draw therefrom strength and refreshment and whatever grace they need in the hardships of life, and especially, at the hour of death. On each day you will bring to My Heart a different group of souls, and you will immerse them in this ocean of My mercy, and I will bring all these souls into the house of My Father. You will do this in this life and in the next. I will deny nothing to any soul whom you will bring to the fount of My mercy. On each day you will beg My Father, on the strength of My bitter Passion, for graces for these souls." (Diary 1209)

First Day

Christ to Saint Faustina: "Today bring to Me all mankind, especially all sinners, and immerse them in the ocean of My mercy. In this way you will console Me in the bitter grief into which the loss of souls plunges Me."

Most Merciful Jesus, whose very nature it is to have compassion on us and to forgive us, do not look upon our sins but upon our trust which we place in Your infinite goodness. Receive us all into the abode of Your Most Compassionate Heart, and never let us escape from It. We beg this of You by Your love which unites You to the Father and the Holy Spirit.

Eternal Father, turn Your merciful gaze upon all mankind and especially upon poor sinners, all enfolded in the Most Compassionate Heart of Jesus. For the sake of His sorrowful Passion show us Your mercy, that we may praise the omnipotence of Your mercy forever and ever. Amen.

(Then pray the Chaplet to the Divine Mercy)

Second Day

Christ to Saint Faustina: **"Today bring to Me the souls of priests and religious, and immerse them in My unfathomable mercy. It was they who gave Me strength to endure My bitter Passion. Through them, as through channels, My mercy flows upon mankind."**

Most Merciful Jesus, from whom comes all that is good, increase Your grace in us, that we may perform worthy works of mercy, consecrated to Your service, that they may perform worthy works of mercy; and that all who see them may glorify the Father of Mercy who is in heaven.

Eternal Father, turn Your merciful gaze upon the company of chosen ones in your vineyard – upon the souls of priests and religious; and endow them with the strength of Your blessing. For the love of the Heart of Your Son in which they are enfolded, impart to them Your power and light, that they may be able to guide others in the way of salvation and with one voice sing praise to Your boundless mercy for ages without end. Amen.

(Then pray the Chaplet to the Divine Mercy)

Third Day

Christ to Saint Faustina: **"Today bring to Me all devout and faithful souls, immerse them in the ocean of My mercy. These souls brought me consolation on the Way of the Cross. They were that drop of consolation in the midst of an ocean of bitterness."**

Most Merciful Jesus, from the treasury of Your mercy, You impart Your graces in great abundance to each and all. Receive us into the abode of Your Most Compassionate Heart and never let us escape from It. We beg this grace of You by that most wondrous love for the heavenly Father with which Your Heart burns so fiercely.

Eternal Father, turn Your merciful gaze upon faithful souls, as upon the inheritance of Your Son. For the sake of His sorrowful Passion, grant them Your blessing and surround them with Your constant protection. Thus may they never fail in love or lose the treasure of the holy faith, but rather, with all the hosts of angels and saints, may they glorify Your boundless mercy for endless ages. Amen.

(Then pray the Chaplet to the Divine Mercy)

Fourth Day

Christ to Saint Faustina: "**Today bring to Me the pagans and those who do not yet know me. I was thinking also of them during My bitter Passion, and their future zeal comforted My Heart. Immerse them in the ocean of My mercy.**"

Most compassionate Jesus, You are the Light of the whole world. Receive into the abode of Your Most Compassionate Heart the souls of pagans who as yet do not know You. Let the rays of Your grace enlighten them that they, too, together with us, may extol Your wonderful mercy; and do not let them escape from the abode which is Your Most Compassionate Heart.

Eternal Father, turn Your merciful gaze upon the souls of pagans and who as yet do not know You, but who are enclosed in the Most Compassionate Heart of Jesus. Draw them to the light of the Gospel. These souls do not know what great happiness it is to love You. Grant that they, too, may extol the generosity of Your mercy for endless ages. Amen.

(Then pray the Chaplet to the Divine Mercy)

Fifth Day

Christ to Saint Faustina: "**Today bring to Me the souls of heretics and schismatics and immerse them in the ocean of My mercy. During My bitter passion they tore at My Body and Heart, that** is, My Church. As they return to unity with the Church, My wounds heal and in this way they alleviate My Passion."

Most Merciful Jesus, Goodness Itself, You do not refuse light to those who seek it of You. Receive into the abode of Your Most Compassionate Heart the souls of heretics and schismatics. Draw them by Your light into the unity of the Church, and do not let them escape from the abode of Your Most Compassionate Heart; but bring it about that they, too, come to glorify the generosity of Your mercy.

Eternal Father, turn Your merciful gaze upon the souls of heretics and schismatics, who have squandered Your blessings and misused Your graces by obstinately persisting in their errors. Do not look upon their errors, but upon the love of Your own Son and upon His bitter Passion, which He underwent for their sake, since they, too, are enclosed in His Most Compassionate Heart of Jesus. Bring it about that they also may glorify Your great mercy for endless ages. Amen.

(Then pray the Chaplet to the Divine Mercy)

Sixth Day
Christ to Saint Faustina: "**Today bring to Me the meek and humble souls and the souls of little children, and immerse them in My mercy. These souls most closely resemble My Heart. They strengthened Me during My bitter agony. I saw them as earthly angels, who will keep vigil at My altars. I pour out upon them whole torrents of grace. Only the humble soul is capable of receiving My grace. I favour humble souls with My confidence.**"

Most Merciful Jesus, You yourself have said, "Learn from Me for I am meek and humble of heart." Receive into the abode of Your Most Compassionate Heart all meek and humble souls and the souls of little children. These souls send all Heaven into ecstasy and they are the heavenly Father's favourites. They are a sweet-smelling bouquet before the throne of God; God Himself takes delight in their fragrance. These souls have a permanent abode in Your Most Compassionate Heart, O Jesus, and they unceasingly sing out a hymn of love and mercy.

Eternal Father, turn Your merciful gaze upon meek and humble souls, and upon little children who are enfolded in the abode which is the Most Compassionate Heart of Jesus. These souls bear the closest resemblance to Your Son. Their fragrance rises from the Earth and reaches Your very throne. Father of mercy and of all goodness., I beg You by the love You bear these souls and by the delight You take in them: Bless the whole world, that all souls together may sing out the praises of Your mercy for endless ages. Amen.

(Then pray the Chaplet to the Divine Mercy)

Seventh Day
Christ to Saint Faustina: "**Today bring to Me the souls who especially venerate and glorify My mercy, and immerse them in My mercy. These souls sorrowed most over my Passion and entered most deeply into My Spirit. They are living images of My Compassionate Heart. These souls will shine with a special brightness in the next life. Not one of them will go into the fire of hell. I shall particularly defend each one of them at the hour of death.**"

Most Merciful Jesus, whose Heart is Love Itself, receive into the abode of Your Most Compassionate Heart the souls of those who particularly extol and venerate the greatness of Your mercy. These souls are mighty with the very power of God Himself. In the midst of all afflictions and adversities they go forward, confident of Your mercy. These souls are united to Jesus and carry all mankind on their shoulders. These souls will not be judged severely, but Your mercy will embrace them as they depart from this life.

Eternal Father, turn Your merciful gaze upon the souls who glorify and venerate Your greatest attribute, that of Your fathomless mercy, and who are enclosed in the Most Compassionate Heart of Jesus. These souls are a living Gospel; their hands are full of deeds of mercy, and their spirits, overflowing with joy, sing a canticle of mercy to You, O Most High! I beg You O God: Show them Your mercy according to the hope and trust they have placed in You. Let there be accomplished in them the promise of Jesus, who said to them, **I Myself will defend as My own glory, during their lifetime, and especially at the hour of their death, those souls who will venerate My fathomless mercy.** Amen.

(Then pray the Chaplet to the Divine Mercy)

Eighth Day
Christ to Saint Faustina: **"Today bring to Me the souls who are in the prison of purgatory, and immerse them in the abyss of My mercy. Let the torrents of My Blood cool down their scorching flames. All these souls are greatly loved by Me. They are making retribution to My justice. It is in your power to bring them relief. Draw all the indulgences from the treasury of My Church and offer them on their behalf. Oh, if you only knew the torments they suffer, you would continually offer for them the alms of the spirit and pay off their debt to My justice."**

Most Merciful Jesus, You Yourself have said that You desire mercy; so I bring into the abode of Your Most Compassionate Heart the souls in purgatory, souls who are very dear to You, and yet, who must make retribution to Your justice. May the streams of blood and water which gushed forth from Your Heart put out the flames of purifying fire, that in the place, too, the power of Your mercy may be praised.

Eternal Father, turn Your merciful gaze upon the souls suffering in purgatory, who are enfolded in the Most Compassionate Heart of Jesus. I beg You, by the sorrowful Passion of Jesus Your Son, and by all the bitterness with which His most sacred Soul was flooded, manifest Your mercy to the souls who are under Your just scrutiny. Look upon them in no other way but only through the wounds of Jesus, Your dearly beloved Son; for we firmly believe that there is no limit to Your goodness and compassion. Amen.

(Then pray the Chaplet to the Divine Mercy)

Ninth Day

Christ to Saint Faustina: **"Today bring to Me souls who have become lukewarm, and immerse them in the abyss of My mercy. These souls wound My Heart most painfully. My soul suffered the most dreadful loathing in the Garden of Olives because of lukewarm souls. They were the reason I cried out: "Father, take this cup away from Me, if it be Your will." For them, the last hope of salvation is flee to My mercy."**

Most compassionate Jesus, You are Compassion Itself. I bring lukewarm souls into the abode of Your Most Compassionate Heart. In this fire of Your pure love, let these tepid souls, who, like corpses, filled You with such deep loathing, be once again set aflame. O Most Compassionate Jesus, exercise the omnipotence of Your mercy and draw them into the very ardour of Your love, and bestow upon them the gift of holy love, for nothing is beyond Your power.

Eternal Father, turn Your merciful gaze upon lukewarm souls who are nonetheless enfolded in the Most Compassionate Heart of Jesus. Father of Mercy, I beg You by the bitter Passion of Your Son and by His three hour agony on the cross: Let them, too, glorify the abyss of Your mercy. Amen.

(Then pray the Chaplet to the Divine Mercy)

Concerning the Feast of Mercy Jesus said:
"Whoever approaches the Fount of Life on this day will be granted complete forgiveness of sins and punishment." (Diary 300).

"I want the image solemnly blessed on the first Sunday after Easter, and I want it to be venerated publicly so that every soul may know about it."(Diary 341)

"This Feast emerged from the very depths of My mercy, and it is confirmed in the vast depths of my tender mercies." (Diary 420)

Saint Faustina later revealed:
"On one occasion, I heard these words: **My daughter, tell the whole world about My inconceivable mercy. I desire that the Feast of Mercy be a refuge and shelter for all souls, and especially for poor sinners. On that day the very depths of My tender mercy are open. I pour out a whole ocean of graces upon those souls who approach the fount of Mercy. The soul that will go to Confession and receive Holy Communion shall obtain complete forgiveness of sins and punishment. On that day all the divine floodgates through which grace flow are opened. Let no soul fear to draw near to Me, even though its sins be as scarlet. My mercy is so great that no mind, be it of man or of angel, will able to fathom it throughout all eternity. Everything that exists has come forth from the very depths of My most tender mercy. Every soul in its relation to Me will contemplate My love and mercy throughout eternity. The Feast of Mercy emerged from My very depths of tenderness. It is My desire that it be solemnly celebrated on the first Sunday after Easter. Mankind will not have peace until it turns to the Fount of My Mercy.**" (Diary 699)

"I demand from you deeds of mercy, which are to arise out of love for Me. You are to show mercy to your neighbours always and everywhere. You must not shrink from this or try to excuse or absolve yourself from it." (Diary 742)

"I want to grant complete pardon to the souls that will go to Confession and receive Holy Communion on the Feast of My mercy." (Diary 1109)

In summary, we must remember that Christ makes extraordinary promises for those who fulfil the conditions for the worthy celebration of the feast. He promises a complete remission of their sins and punishment. This means that, provided they have trust in God's goodness, show active love towards their neighbour and die in a state of sanctifying grace (confession and worthy reception of Communion), they will go straight to heaven without going through the purgative fire of purgatory.

The Image of the Divine Mercy

On 22nd February 1931, Jesus appeared to Saint Faustina with two rays of light radiating from His heart (a pale ray and a red ray). Jesus said: "Paint an image according to the pattern you see, with the signature: Jesus I trust in You. I desire that this image be venerated, first in your chapel and throughout the world." (Diary 47)

"I promise that the soul that will venerate this image will not perish. I also promise victory over its enemies already here on Earth, especially at the hour of death. I myself will defend it as My own glory." (Diary 48)

"I am offering people a vessel with which they are to keep coming for graces to the fountain of mercy. That vessel is this image with the signature: Jesus, I trust in You." (Diary 327)

"The two rays denote Blood and Water. The pale ray stands for the Water which makes souls righteous. The red ray stands for the Blood which is the life of souls. These two rays issued forth from the very depths of My tender mercy when My agonized Heart was opened by a lance on the Cross. These rays shield souls from the wrath of My Father. Happy is the one who dwells in their shelter, for the just hand of God shall not lay hold of him." (Diary 299)

"Not in the beauty of the colour, nor of the brush lies the greatness of this image, but in My grace." (Diary 313)

"By means of this image I shall grant many graces to souls. It is to be a reminder of the demands of My mercy, because even the strongest faith is of no avail without works." (Diary 742)

When Christ calls upon us to venerate the Image of the Divine Mercy, He is not asking us to venerate the painting itself but rather He wants us to be led to the mysteries to which the image leads us or what it represents. The image is a vessel that reminds us of God's mercy. This image is revealing to us a fountain of graces flowing from the pierced Heart of Christ on the Cross. The water represents baptism, the gift of the Spirit which cleanses us of all our sins and the blood represents the Eucharist, Christ's gift of Himself to the Father to expiate our sins on the cross. So, the image of the pierced side of Christ pouring out blood and water reminds us that the Cross is the price of mercy. The image should help us to remember the terrible price paid to redeem us. Looking at the image, we should be distressed with St Teresa of Avila who in contemplation of God saw the extent of human ingratitude and put it as follows: "What has become of Christians now? Must those who owe you most always be those who distress you?" If we are able to look at the image with faith and trust, the Spirit will interiorly reveal the secrets of the water and blood and make us aware of our own sins and the mercy of God.

Christ promises to those who look at the image with eyes of faith eternal salvation and progress in Christian perfection. He promises the grace of a happy death and all other graces which people will ask of Him with trust.

The Chaplet of Divine Mercy

In reciting the Chaplet, we are offering to God the Body, Blood, Soul and Divinity of our Lord Jesus Christ. We are affirming our belief that all our good actions can only proceed from the obedience and sacrifices of Christ which have been accepted by His Father. The Holy Spirit therefore draws from the treasures of Christ's sacrifices the gifts that enable us to have great merits before God, to become co-heirs with Christ and worthy of eternal life. So it is the glorified Body of Christ that we behold during the recitation of the Chaplet. But we are also reminded that it was through His Blood of sacrifice that showed the Father's love for His Son and how pleased He was with His obedience and sacrifice. The Chaplet is therefore a prayer of atonement which reconciles us to God and unites us to the sacrifice of Christ. It is a prayer that was dictated by Christ Himself to Saint Faustina. When reciting the prayer, we are called upon to trust in God's mercy, to show humility and believe in the efficacy of Christ's redemptive act.

Christ promised Saint Faustina that all those who prayed the Chaplet would receive the grace of conversion and have a peaceful death. He also promised that if the Chaplet is recited at the side of a dying person, he will have a peaceful death.

The Chaplet

1   Begin with the Sign of the Cross, 1 Our Father, 1 Hail Mary and The Apostles Creed.
2   Then on the Our Father Beads say the following: Eternal Father, I offer You the Body and Blood, Soul and Divinity of Your dearly beloved Son, Our Lord Jesus Christ, in atonement for our sins and those of the whole world.
3   On the 10 Hail Mary Beads say the following: For the sake of His sorrowful Passion, have mercy on us and on the whole world.
    (Repeat step 2 and 3 for all five decades)
4   Conclude with (three times): Holy God, Holy Mighty One, Holy Immortal One, have mercy on us and on the whole world.

The Hour of Mercy

Jesus asked Saint Faustina and through Saint Faustina, for us, to celebrate this hour of great mercy, promising great graces to those who do this for themselves and on behalf of other people.

"At three o'clock, implore My mercy, especially for sinners; and, if only for a brief moment, immerse yourself in My Passion, particularly in My abandonment at the moment of agony. This is the hour of great mercy for the whole world... In this hour I will refuse nothing to the soul that makes a request of Me in virtue of My Passion."(Diary 1320).

"As often as you hear the clock strike the third hour immerse yourself completely in My mercy, adoring and glorifying it; invoke its omnipotence for the whole world, and particularly for poor sinners, for at that moment mercy was opened wide for every soul. In this hour you can obtain everything for yourself and for others for the asking; it was the hour of grace for the whole world — mercy triumphed over justice."

Try your best to make the Stations of the Cross in this hour, provided that your duties permit it; and if you are not able to make the Stations of the Cross, then at least step into the chapel for a moment and adore, in the most Blessed Sacrament. My Heart, which is full of mercy: and should you be unable to step into chapel. immerse yourself in prayer there where you happen to be, if only for a very brief instant." (Diary 1572)

3 O'clock Prayers

You expired, Jesus, but the source of life gushed forth for souls and the ocean of mercy opened up for the whole world. O Fount of Life, unfathomable Divine Mercy, envelop the whole world and empty Yourself out upon us.

O blood and water, which gushed forth from the Heart of Jesus as a fount of mercy for us, I trust in You.

St Faustina's Way of the Cross: opening prayer

Merciful Lord, my Master, I want to follow You faithfully. I want to imitate You in my life in an ever more perfect way. That is why I ask that by meditating on Your Passion, You would grant me the grace of a deeper understanding of the mysteries of the spiritual life. Mary, Mother of Mercy, always faithful to Christ, lead me in the footsteps of the sorrowful Passion of your Son and ask for me the necessary graces for a fruitful making of this Way of the Cross

Sung verse:

> At the cross her station keeping
> Stood the mournful Mother weeping
> Close to Jesus to the last

First Station: Jesus is condemned to die
Celebrant:
We adore You, O Christ, and we praise You.

People:
Because by Your holy Cross and Resurrection, You have redeemed the world.

Celebrant:
The chief priests and the entire Sanhedrin kept trying to obtain false testimony against Jesus in order to put Him to death, but they found none, though many false witnesses came forward (Matthew 26:59–60).

Jesus: (Celebrant)
Do not be surprised that you are sometimes unjustly accused. I Myself first drank this cup of undeserved suffering for love of you (289). When I was before Herod, I obtained a grace

for you; namely, that you would be able to rise above human scorn and follow faithfully in My footsteps (1164).

S. Faustina: (People)
We are sensitive to words and quickly want to answer back, without taking any regard as to whether it is God's will that we should speak. A silent soul is strong; no adversities will harm it if it perseveres in silence. The silent soul is capable of attaining the closest union with God (477).

All:
Merciful Jesus, help me to know how to accept every human judgment and do not allow me ever to render a condemnatory judgment on You in my neighbours.

Celebrant:
You, who suffered wounds for us,

People:
Christ Jesus, have mercy on us.

Sung verse:
> Through her heart, His sorrow sharing
> All His bitter anguish bearing
> Now at length the sword has passed

Second Station: Jesus carries His cross
Celebrant:
We adore You, O Christ, and we praise You.

People:
Because by Your holy Cross and Resurrection, You have redeemed the world.

Celebrant:
Then Pilate took Jesus and had Him scourged. And the soldiers

wove a crown out of thorns and placed it on His head, and clothed Him in a purple cloak, and they came to Him and said, "Hail, King of the Jews!"

So Jesus came out, wearing the crown of thorns and the purple cloak. And Pilate said to them, "Behold, the man!" When the chief priests and the guards saw Him they cried out, "Crucify Him, crucify Him!" (John 19:1-6).

Jesus: (Celebrant)

Do not be afraid of sufferings; I am with you (151). The more you will come to love suffering, the purer your love for Me will be (279).

S. Faustina: (People)

Jesus, I thank You for the little daily crosses, for opposition to my endeavours, for the hardships of communal life, for the misinterpretation of my intentions, for humiliations at the hands of others, for the harsh way in which we are treated, for false suspicions, for poor health and loss of strength, for self-denial, for dying to myself, for lack of recognition in everything, for the upsetting of all my plans (343).

All:

Merciful Jesus, teach me to value life's toil, sicknesses, and every suffering, and with love to carry my daily crosses.

Celebrant:

You, who suffered wounds for us,

People:

Christ Jesus, have mercy on us.

Sung verse:

> O, how sad and sore distressed
> Was that Mother highly blessed
> of the sole Begotten One.

Third Station: Jesus falls the first time

Celebrant:
We adore You, O Christ, and we praise You.

People:
Because by Your holy Cross and Resurrection, You have redeemed the world.

Celebrant:
We had all gone astray like sheep, each following his own way; But the Lord laid upon Him the guilt of us all (Isaiah 53:6,12).

Jesus: (Celebrant)
Involuntary offences of souls do not hinder My love for them or prevent Me from uniting Myself with them. But voluntary offences, even the smallest, obstruct My graces, and I cannot lavish My gifts on such souls (1641).

S. Faustina: (People)
My Jesus, despite Your graces, I see and feel all my misery...O my Jesus, how prone I am to evil, and this forces me to be constantly vigilant. But I do not lose heart. I trust God's grace, which abounds in the worst misery (606).

All:
Merciful Lord, preserve me from every, even the tiniest but voluntary and conscious infidelity.

Celebrant:
You, who suffered wounds for us,

People:
Christ Jesus, have mercy on us.

Sung verse:

> Is there one who would not weep,
> Whelmed in miseries so deep
> Christ's dear Mother to behold?

Fourth Station: Jesus meets His sorrowful mother

Celebrant:

We adore You, O Christ, and we praise You.

People:

Because by Your holy Cross and Resurrection, You have redeemed the world.

Celebrant:

Behold, this child is destined for the fall and rise of many in Israel, and to be a sign that will be contradicted so that the thoughts of many hearts may be revealed. And you yourself a sword will pierce (Luke 2:34–35).

Jesus: (Celebrant)

Although all the works that come into being by My will are exposed to great sufferings, consider whether any of them has been subject to greater difficulties than that work which is directly Mine – the work of Redemption. You should not worry too much about adversities. (1643).

S. Faustina: (People)

I saw the Blessed Virgin, unspeakably beautiful. She held me close to herself and said to me, I am Mother to you all, thanks to the unfathomable mercy of God. Most pleasing to me is that soul which faithfully carries out the will of God. Be courageous. Do not fear apparent obstacles, but fix your gaze upon the Passion of my Son, and in this way you will be victorious (449).

All:
Mary, Mother of Mercy, be near me always, especially in suffering as you were on your Son's Way of the Cross.

Celebrant:
You, who suffered wounds for us,

People:
Christ Jesus, have mercy on us.

Sung verse:
> Can the human heart refrain
> From partaking in her pain
> In that Mother's pain untold?

Fifth Station: Simon helps Jesus carry His cross
Celebrant:
We adore You, O Christ, and we praise You.

People:
Because by Your holy Cross and Resurrection, You have redeemed the world.

Celebrant:
As they led Him away they took hold of a certain Simon, a Cyrenian, who was coming in from the country; and after laying the cross on him, they made him carry it behind Jesus (Luke 23:26).

Jesus: (Celebrant)
Write that by day and by night My gaze is fixed upon him, and I permit these adversities in order to increase his merit. I do not reward for good results but for the patience and hardship undergone for My sake (86).

S. Faustina: (People)

Jesus, You do not give a reward for the successful performance of a work, but for the good will and the labour undertaken. Therefore, I am completely at peace, even if all my undertakings and efforts should be thwarted or should come to naught. If I do all that is in my power, the rest is not my business (952).

All:

Jesus, my Lord, let my every thought, word, and deed be undertaken exclusively out of love for You. Keep on cleansing my intentions.

Celebrant:

You, who suffered wounds for us,

People:

Christ Jesus, have mercy on us.

Sung verse:

> Let me share with thee His pain
> Who for all my sins was slain,
> Who for me in torments died.

Sixth Station: Veronica wipes the face of Jesus

Celebrant:

We adore You, O Christ, and we praise You.

People:

Because by Your holy Cross and Resurrection, You have redeemed the world.

Celebrant:

He grew up like a sapling before him, like a shoot from the parched Earth; There was in Him no stately bearing to make us look at

Him, no appearance that would attract us to Him. He was spurned and avoided by men, a Man of suffering, accustomed to infirmity. One of those from whom men hide their faces spurned, and we held Him in no esteem (Isaiah 53:2-3).

Jesus: (Celebrant)
Know that whatever good you do to any soul, I accept it as if you had done it to Me (1768).

S. Faustina: (People)
I am learning how to be good from Jesus, from Him who is goodness itself, so that I may be called a [child] of the heavenly Father (669). Great love can change small things into great ones, and it is only love which lends value to our actions (303).

All:
Lord Jesus, my Master, grant that my eyes, my hands, my lips and my heart may always be merciful. Transform me into mercy.

Celebrant:
You, who suffered wounds for us,

People:
Christ Jesus, have mercy on us.

Sung verse:
> Let me mingle tears with thee,
> Mourning Him who mourned for me,
> All the days that I may live.

Seventh Station: Jesus falls the second time
Celebrant:
We adore You, O Christ, and we praise You.

People:

Because by Your holy Cross and Resurrection, You have redeemed the world.

Celebrant:

Yet it was our infirmities that He bore, our sufferings that He endured, while we thought of Him as stricken, as one smitten by God and afflicted (Isaiah 53:4).

Jesus: (Celebrant)

The cause of your falls is that you rely too much upon yourself and too little on Me. But let this not sadden you so much. You are dealing with the God of mercy (1488). Know that of yourself you can do nothing (639). Without special help from Me, you are not even capable of accepting My graces (738).

S. Faustina: (People)

Jesus, do not leave me alone in suffering. You know, Lord, how weak I am. I am an abyss of wretchedness, I am nothingness itself; so what will be so strange if You leave me alone and I fall? (1489). So You, Jesus, must stand by me constantly like a mother by a helpless child – and even more so (264).

All:

May Your grace assist me, Lord, that I may not keep falling continuously into the same faults; and when I fall, help me to rise and glorify Your mercy.

Celebrant:

You, who suffered wounds for us,

People:

Christ Jesus, have mercy on us.

Sung verse:
>Make me feel as thou hast felt;
>Make my soul to glow and melt
>With the love of Christ my Lord

Eighth Station: Jesus meets the women of Jerusalem
Celebrant:
We adore You, O Christ, and we praise You.

People:
Because by Your holy Cross and Resurrection, You have redeemed the world.

Celebrant:
A large crowd of people followed Jesus, including many women who mourned and lamented Him. Jesus turned to them and said, "Daughters of Jerusalem, do not weep for Me; weep instead for yourselves and for your children (Luke 23:27-28).

Jesus: (Celebrant)
O how pleasing to Me is living faith! (1420). Tell all, that I demand that they live in the spirit of faith (353).

S. Faustina: (People)
I fervently beg the Lord to strengthen my faith, so that in my drab, everyday life I will not be guided by human dispositions, but by those of the spirit. Oh, how everything drags Man towards the Earth! But lively faith maintains the soul in the higher regions and assigns self-love its proper place; that is to say, the lowest one (210).

All:
Merciful Lord, I thank You for holy Baptism and the grace of faith. Continuously, I call: Lord, I believe, increase my faith.

Celebrant:
You, who suffered wounds for us,

People:
Christ Jesus, have mercy on us.

Sung verse:
> O thou Mother! Fount of love!
> Touch my spirit from above,
> Make my heart with thine accord.

Ninth Station: Jesus falls the third time
Celebrant:
We adore You, O Christ, and we praise You.

People:
Because by Your holy Cross and Resurrection, You have redeemed the world.

Celebrant:
Though He was harshly treated, He submitted and opened not His mouth. Like a lamb led to the slaughter or a sheep before the shearers, He was silent and opened not His mouth. Oppressed and condemned, though He had done no wrong nor spoken any falsehood. But the Lord was pleased to crush Him in infirmity. Because of His affliction He shall see the light in fulness of days (Isaiah 53:7-10).

Jesus: (Celebrant)
My child, know that the greatest obstacles to holiness are discouragement and an exaggerated anxiety. These will deprive you of the ability to practice virtue. Do not lose heart in coming for pardon, for I am always ready to forgive you. As often as you beg for it, you glorify My mercy (1488).

S. Faustina: (People)
My Jesus, despite Your graces, I see and feel all my misery. I begin my day with battle and end it with battle. As soon as I conquer one obstacle, ten more appear to take its place. But I am not worried, because I know that this is the time of struggle, not peace (606).

All:
Merciful Lord, I give over to You that which is my exclusive property, that is, my sin and my human weakness. I beg You, may my misery drown in Your unfathomable mercy.

Celebrant:
You, who suffered wounds for us,

People:
Christ Jesus, have mercy on us.

Sung verse:
> Wounded with His ev'ry wound
> Steep my soul till it hath swooned
> In His very Blood away.

Tenth Station: Jesus is stripped of His garments
Celebrant:
We adore You, O Christ, and we praise You.

People:
Because by Your holy Cross and Resurrection, You have redeemed the world.

Celebrant:
When the soldiers had crucified Jesus, they took His clothes and divided them into four shares, a share for each soldier. They also took His tunic, but the tunic was seamless, woven in one piece

from the top down. So they said to one another, "Let's not tear it, but cast lots for it to see whose it will be," in order that the passage of scripture might be fulfilled (John 19:23-24).

S. Faustina: (People)
Jesus was suddenly standing before me, stripped of His clothes, His Body completely covered with wounds, His eyes flooded with tears and blood, His face disfigured and covered with spittle.

Jesus: (Celebrant)
The bride must resemble her betrothed.

S. Faustina: (People)
I understood these words to their very depth. There is no room for doubt here. My likeness to Jesus must be through suffering and humility (268).

All:
Jesus, meek and humble of heart, make my heart like unto Your heart.

Celebrant:
You, who suffered wounds for us,

People:
Christ Jesus, have mercy on us.

Sung verse:
> Bruised, derided, cursed, defiled,
> She beheld her tender Child
> All with bloody scourges rent

Eleventh Station: Jesus is nailed to the cross
Celebrant:
We adore You, O Christ, and we praise You.

People:
Because by Your holy Cross and Resurrection, You have redeemed the world.

Celebrant:
Those passing by reviled Him, shaking their heads and saying, "You would destroy the temple and rebuild it in three days, save Yourself, if You are the Son of God, [and] come down from the cross!" Likewise the chief priests with the scribes and elders mocked Him and said, "He saved others; He cannot save Himself. He trusted in God; let Him deliver Him now if he wants Him. For He said, 'I am the Son of God'" (Matthew 27:39–43).

Jesus: (Celebrant)
My pupil, have great love for those who cause you suffering. Do good to those who hate you (1628).

S. Faustina: (People)
O my Jesus, You know what efforts are needed to live sincerely and unaffectedly with those from whom our nature flees, or with those who, deliberately or not, have made us suffer. Humanly speaking, this is impossible. At such times more than at others, I try to discover the Lord Jesus in such a person and for the same Jesus, I do everything for such people (766).

All:
O purest Love, rule in all Your plenitude in my heart and help me to do Your holy will most faithfully (328).

Celebrant:
You, who suffered wounds for us,

People:
Christ Jesus, have mercy on us.

Sung verse:

> Holy Mother! pierce me through;
> In my heart each wound renew
> Of my Saviour crucified.

Twelfth Station: Jesus dies on the cross

Celebrant:

We adore You, O Christ, and we praise You.

People:

Because by Your holy Cross and Resurrection, You have redeemed the world.

Celebrant:

But when they came to Jesus and saw that He was already dead, they did not break His legs, but one soldier thrust his lance into His side, and immediately blood and water flowed out (John 19:33-40).

Jesus: (Celebrant)

All this is for the salvation of souls. Consider well, My daughter, what you are doing for their salvation (1184).

S. Faustina: (People)

Then I saw the Lord Jesus nailed to the cross. When He had hung on it for a while, I saw a multitude of souls crucified like Him. Then I saw a second multitude of souls, and a third. The second multitude were not nailed to [their] crosses, but were holding them firmly in their hands. The third were neither nailed to [their] crosses nor holding them firmly in their hands, but were dragging [their] crosses behind them and were discontent.

Jesus: (Celebrant)

Do you see these souls? Those who are like Me in the pain and contempt they suffer will be like Me also in glory. And

those who resemble Me less in pain and contempt will also bear less resemblance to Me in glory (446).

All:
Jesus, my Saviour, hide me in the depth of Your heart that, fortified by Your grace, I may be able to resemble You in the love of the Cross and have a share in Your glory.

Celebrant:
You, who suffered wounds for us,

People:
Christ Jesus, have mercy on us.

Sung verse:
>   For the sins of His own nation,
>   Saw Him hang in desolation
>   Till His Spirit forth He sent

Thirteenth Station: Jesus is taken down from the Cross
Celebrant:
We adore You, O Christ, and we praise You.

People:
Because by Your holy Cross and Resurrection, You have redeemed the world.

Celebrant:
The centurion who witnessed what had happened glorified God and said, "This man was innocent beyond doubt." When all the people who had gathered for this spectacle saw what had happened, they returned home beating their breasts; but all His acquaintances stood at a distance, including the women who had followed Him from Galilee, and saw these events (Luke 23:47-49).

Jesus: (Celebrant)
Most dear to Me is the soul that strongly believes in My goodness and has complete trust in Me. I heap My confidence upon it and give it all it asks (453).

S. Faustina: (People)
I fly to Your mercy, Compassionate God, who alone are good. Although my misery is great, and my offenses are many, I trust in Your mercy, because You are the God of mercy; and, from time immemorial, it has never been heard of, nor do heaven or earth remember, that a soul trusting in Your mercy has been disappointed (1730).

All:
Merciful Jesus, daily increase my trust in Your mercy that always and everywhere I may give witness to Your boundless goodness and love.

Celebrant:
You, who suffered wounds for us,

People:
Christ Jesus, have mercy on us.

Sung verse:
> Virgin of all virgins blest!
> Listen to my fond request:
> Let me share your grief divine

Fourteenth Station: Jesus is placed in the sepulchre
Celebrant:
We adore You, O Christ, and we praise You.

People:
Because by Your holy Cross and Resurrection, You have redeemed the world.

Celebrant:

They took the Body of Jesus and bound It with burial cloths along with the spices, according to the Jewish burial custom. Now in the place where He had been crucified there was a garden, and in the garden a new tomb, in which no one had yet been buried. So they laid Jesus there because of the Jewish preparation day; for the tomb was close by (John 19:38–42).

Jesus: (Celebrant)

But child, you are not yet in your homeland; so go, fortified by My grace, and fight for My kingdom in human souls; fight as a king's child would; and remember that the days of your exile will pass quickly, and with them the possibility of earning merit for heaven. I expect from you, My child, a great number of souls who will glorify My mercy for all eternity (1489).

S. Faustina: (People)

Every soul You have entrusted to me, Jesus, I will try to aid with prayer and sacrifice, so that Your grace can work in them. O great lover of souls, my Jesus, I thank You for this immense confidence with which You have deigned to place souls in our care (245).

All:

Grant, Merciful Lord, that not even one of those souls which You have entrusted to me be lost.

Celebrant:

You, who suffered wounds for us,

People:

Christ Jesus, have mercy on us.

Sung verse:

> Christ, when Thou shalt call me hence,
> Be Thy Mother my defence,
> Be Thy Cross my victory

All:

My Jesus, my only hope, I thank You for this book which You opened to the eyes of my soul. This book is Your Passion, undertaken out of love for me. From this book, I learn how to love God and souls. This book contains inexhaustible treasures. O Jesus, how few souls understand You in Your martyrdom of love. Happy the soul that has come to understand the love of the heart of Jesus!

For the intentions of the Holy Father

Our Father...Hail Mary...Glory Be...

Prayer in Honor of the Holy Cross:
God our Father, in obedience to You Your only Son accepted death on the cross for the salvation of mankind. We acknowledge the mystery of the cross on earth. May we receive the gift of redemption in Heaven. We ask this through our Lord Jesus Christ, Your Son, Who lives and reigns with You and the Holy Spirit one God, for ever and ever. Amen.

(Sung verses taken from the hymn, *Stabat Mater*)

Prayers that will be beneficial during The Hour of Mercy

The Fifteen Prayers Revealed by Our Lord to St Bridget of Sweden in the Church of St Paul, Rome

As St Bridget knelt before the Crucifix, above the Tabernacle in the Blessed Sacrament Chapel, she received fifteen prayers from Our Lord Jesus Christ. The crucifix is still displayed in St Paul Church in Rome. The inscription placed in the church reads as follows: "Pendentis pendent Dei verba accepitaure accipit at verbum corde Brigitta Deum. Anno Junilei MCCCCL," which recalls the mystery of the crucifix conversing with St Bridget. "Bridget not only receives the words of God hanging in the air, but takes the Word of God into her heart. Jubilee Year 1350."

The Prayers will be extremely useful as a basis for meditation during the Hour of Mercy.

Pope Pius IX approved the prayers on 31st May 1862, as true and for the good of souls.

First Prayer
Our Father – Hail Mary. O Jesus Christ! Eternal Sweetness to those who love You, joy surpassing all joy and all desire, salvation and hope of all sinners, You have proved that You have no greater desire than to be among men, even assuming human nature at the fulness of time for the love of men, recall all the sufferings You have endured from the instant of Your conception, and especially during Your Passion, as it was decreed and ordained from all eternity in the Divine plan.

Remember, O Lord, that during the Last Supper with Your disciples, having washed their feet, You gave them Your Most Precious Body and Blood, and while at the same time You did sweetly console them, You did foretell of Your coming Passion.

Remember, the sadness and bitterness which You did experience in Your Soul as You Yourself bore witness saying: "My Soul is sorrowful even unto death."

Remember all the fear, anguish and pain that You did suffer in Your delicate Body before the torment of the Crucifixion, when, after having prayed three times, bathed in a sweat of blood, You were betrayed by Judas, Your disciple, arrested by the people of a nation You had chosen and elevated, accused by false witnesses, unjustly judged by their judges during the flower of Your youth and during the solemn paschal season.

Remember that You were despoiled of Your garments and clothed in those of derision; that Your Face and Eyes were veiled, that You were buffeted, crowned with thorns, a reed placed in Your Hands, that You were crushed with blows and overwhelmed with affronts and outrages.

In memory of all these pains and sufferings which You did endure before Your Passion on the Cross, grant me before my death true contrition, a sincere and entire confession, worthy satisfaction and the remission of all my sins. Amen.

Second Prayer
Our Father – Hail Mary. O Jesus! True liberty of angels, Paradise of delights, remember the horror and sadness which You did endure when Your enemies, like furious lions, surrounded You, and by thousands of insults, spits, blows, lacerations and other unheard-of – cruelties, tormented You at will. In consideration of these torments and insulting words, I beseech You, O my Saviour, to deliver me from all my enemies visible and invisible and to bring me, under Your protection, to the perfection of eternal salvation, Amen.

Third Prayer
Our Father – Hail Mary. O Jesus! Creator of Heaven and Earth Whom nothing can encompass or limit, You Who do enfold and hold all under Your Loving power, remember the very bitter pain You did suffer when the Jews nailed Your Sacred Hands and Feet to the Cross by blow after blow with big blunt nails, and not finding You in a pitiable enough state to satisfy their rage, they enlarged Your Wounds, and added pain to pain, and with indescribable cruelty stretched Your Body on the Cross, pulled You from all sides, thus dislocating Your Limbs. I beg of You, O Jesus, by the memory of this most loving suffering of the Cross, to grant me the grace to fear You and to Love You. Amen.

Fourth Prayer
Our Father – Hail Mary. O Jesus! Heavenly Physician, raised aloft on the Cross to heal our wounds with Yours, remember the bruises which You did suffer and the weakness of all Your members which were distended to such a degree that never was there pain like Yours. From the crown on your Head to the Soles of Your Feet there was not one spot on Your Body that was not in torment, and yet,

forgetting all Your sufferings, You did not cease to pray to Your Heavenly Father for Your enemies saying: "Father forgive them for they know not what they do."

Through this great Mercy, and in memory of this suffering, grant that the remembrance of Your Most Bitter Passion may effect in us a perfect contrition and the remission of all our sins. Amen.

Fifth Prayer

Our Father – Hail Mary. O Jesus! Mirror of eternal splendour, remember the sadness which You experienced, when contemplating in the light of Your Divinity and predestination of those who would be saved by the merits of Your Sacred Passion, You did see at the same time, the great multitude of reprobates who would be damned for their sins, and You did complain bitterly of those hopeless lost and unfortunate sinners. Through this abyss of compassion and pity, and especially through the goodness which You displayed to the good thief when You said to him: "This day, You shall be with Me in Paradise." I beg of You, O Sweet Jesus, that at the hour of my death, You will show me mercy too. Amen.

Sixth Prayer

Our Father – Hail Mary. O Jesus! Beloved and most desirable King, remember the grief You did suffer, when naked and like a common criminal, You were fastened and raised on the Cross, when all Your relatives and friends abandoned You, except Your Beloved Mother, who remained close to You during Your agony and whom You did entrust to Your faithful disciple when You said to Mary: "Woman, behold your son!" And to St John: "Son, behold Your Mother!"

I beg of You O my Saviour, by the sword of sorrow which pierced the soul of Your holy Mother, to have compassion on me in all my afflictions and tribulations, both corporal and spiritual, and to assist me in all my trials, and especially at the hour of my death. Amen.

Seventh Prayer

Our Father – Hail Mary. O Jesus! Inexhaustible Fountain of compassion, Who by a profound gesture of Love, said from the Cross: "I thirst", suffered with a thirst for the salvation of the human race. I beg of You O my Saviour, to inflame in our hearts the desire to tend towards perfection in all our acts; and to extinguish in us the excessive desire of the flesh and the love of worldly things. Amen.

Eighth Prayer

Our Father – Hail Mary. O Jesus! Sweetness of Hearts, delight of the spirit, by the bitterness of the vinegar and gall which You did taste on the Cross for Love of us, grant us the grace to receive worthily Your Precious Body and Blood during our life and at the hour of our death, that they may serve as a remedy and consolation for our souls. Amen.

Ninth Prayer

Our Father – Hail Mary. O Jesus! Royal virtue, joy of the mind, recall the pain You did endure when, plunged in an ocean of bitterness at the approach of death, insulted and outraged, You did cry out in a loud voice that You were abandoned by Your Father, saying "My God, My God, why hast thou forsaken me? Through this anguish, I beg of You, O my Saviour, not to abandon me in the terrors and pains of my death. Amen.

Tenth Prayer

Our Father – Hail Mary. O Jesus! Who art the beginning and end of all things, life and virtue, remember that for our sakes You were plunged in an abyss of suffering from the soles of Your Feet to the crown of Your Head. In consideration of the enormity of Your Wounds, teach me to keep, through pure love, Your Commandments, whose way are wide and easy for those who love you. Amen.

Eleventh Prayer

Our Father – Hail Mary. O Jesus! Deep abyss of mercy, I beg of You, in memory of Your Wounds which penetrated to the very marrow of Your Bones and to the depth of Your Being, to draw me, a miserable sinner, overwhelmed by my offences, away from sin and to hide me from Your Face, justly irritated against me, hide me in Your Wounds, until Your anger and just indignation shall have passed away. Amen.

Twelfth Prayer

Our Father – Hail Mary. O Jesus! Mirror of Truth, Symbol of Unity, Link of Charity, remember the multitude of wounds with which You were covered from head to foot, torn and reddened by the spilling of Your adorable Blood. O Great and Universal Pain which You did suffer in Your virginal Flesh for Love of us! Sweetest Jesus! What is there that You could have done for us which You have not done? May the fruit of Your sufferings be renewed in my soul by the faithful remembrance of Your Passion and may Your Love increase in my heart each day, until I see You in eternity.

You who are the treasury of every real good and every joy, which I beg You to grant me, O Sweetest Jesus, in Heaven, Amen.

Thirteenth Prayer

Our Father – Hail Mary. O Jesus! Strong Lion, Immortal and Invincible King, remember the pain which You did endure when all Your strength, both moral and physical, was entirely exhausted, You did bow Your Head, saying: "It is consummated." Through this anguish and grief, I beg of You Lord Jesus, to have mercy on me at the hour of my death when my mind will be greatly troubled and my soul will be in anguish. Amen.

Fourteenth Prayer

Our Father – Hail Mary. O Jesus! Only Son of the Father, Splendour and Figure of His Substance, remember the simple and humble recommendation You did make of Your Soul to Your Eternal Father, saying: "Father, into Your Hands I commend my Spirit!" And with Your Body all torn, and Your Heart broken, and the bowels of Your Mercy open to redeem us, You did Expire. By this Precious Death,

I beg of You O King of Saints, comfort me and help me to resist the Devil, the flesh and the world, so that being dead to the world I may live for You alone. I beg of You at the hour of my death to receive me, a pilgrim and an exile returning to You. Amen.

Fifteenth Prayer

Our Father – Hail Mary. O Jesus! True and fruitful Vine! Remember the abundant outpouring of Blood which You did so generously shed from Your Sacred Body as juice from grapes in a wine press. From Your Side, pierced with a lance by a soldier, blood and water issued forth until there was not left in Your Body a single drop, and finally, like a bundle of myrrh lifted to the top of the Cross your delicate Flesh was destroyed, the very Substance of Your Body withered, and the Marrow of Your Bones dried up. Through this bitter Passion and through the outpouring of Your Precious Blood, I beg of You, O Sweet Jesus, to receive my soul when I am in my death agony. Amen.

Conclusion

O Sweet Jesus! Pierce my heart so that my tears of penitence and love will be my bread day and night; may I be converted entirely to You, may my heart be Your perpetual habitation, may my conversation be pleasing to You, and may the end of my life be so praiseworthy that I may merit Heaven and there with Your saints, praise You forever. Amen.

The spread of the Divine Mercy Devotion

Jesus said: "Do whatever is within your power to spread devotion to My mercy. I will make up for what you lack. (Diary 1074)

"Souls who spread the honor of My mercy I shield through their entire lives as a tender mother her Infant, and at the hour of death I will not be a Judge for them, but the Merciful Saviour." (Diary 1075) Christ promised to Saint Faustina that those who spread the devotion would be given graces and assistance at the hour of death.

Those who spread the devotion were given graces and assistance at the hour of death.

Novena to the Sacred Heart of Jesus

First Day

God Our Father, as we prepare ourselves for the feast of the Sacred Heart of Jesus, Your Son, We beg You to remove from our minds all darkness, so as to enable us, by the light of Your Holy Spirit to understand the wonderful gifts of mercy that are pouring on mankind through the heart of Jesus. Father, You created us in love for Yourself and it was Your wish that we share Your divinity. We thank You that even when we sin, You did not abandon Your purpose for mankind but through the sacrifice of Your Son, You called us through Your mercy to a new life in the kingdom of heaven. By the institution of the Heart of Jesus, You have shown us the centre of Your love for mankind and You pour through that heart all the graces necessary for redemption. As we prepare for the feast of the heart of Your son, bless all those who seek Your mercies through this devotion and bring them to true repentance through reparation for their sins and contempt for the Devil, the world and the flesh. May the reign of the Heart of Jesus and the Immaculate Heart of Mary cleanse all faithful souls from their sins and lead them to eternal life.

Second Day

Lord Jesus Christ, through the cross, You gave all Your life to mankind and You showed this love through the gift of the Eucharist. We are sorry that through the frequent reception of the Eucharist, we have failed to reflect in the meaning of Your gift and we have also failed to ensure that we receive this gift worthily. As we contemplate the Heart of Jesus and the gifts that Your pierced heart continues to pour gifts on mankind, we beg You to infuse into our souls through repentance for all the offences we have committed against Your heart of love.

Most Sacred Heart of Jesus, we place all our trust in You.

Third Day

Oh Sacred Heart of Jesus, we pray that all families will contemplate the image of Your heart and reflect on the Heart of Jesus as the true source of peace in families. Through devotion to the Heart of Jesus, may we submit fully to the will of God the Father, our Creator, so that we may find true peace and harmony in our families. We are sorry that we have marginalized the commandments of God and look for happiness from riches, worldly honours and pride. Through the Heart of Jesus, may we have the eyes to see that the pleasures and ambitions of this world have led families and neighbours to gossips, power struggles, bitterness, hatred, which have all put people on the road to eternal death.

Oh Heart of Jesus, may we have time to listen to Your interior voice which will lead us to true peace in our own hearts and help us to lead the kind of lives that will unite our hearts to Your Heart. May the Holy Family of Nazareth be a model for all families to imitate. May they see the simplicity of Saint Joseph who found riches in doing God's will and protecting the vulnerable God–child. May families also behold the humility of the Blessed Virgin Mary whose only joy was being united to her Son in body and soul. Finally, we thank God for giving us a Son in human form and presenting Him as a model of a child obedient to His parents and Whose heart became the source of true peace in the family.

Fourth Day

Sacred Heart of Jesus, pierced with a spear to pour on mankind the gifts of the water, of the spirit and the blood of redemption and to atone for our sins. Help us in our moments of temptations and trials, to learn how to bear our crosses. May we find consolation in the Heart of Jesus whenever we go through trials and temptations. May the outpouring of graces from Your Sacred Heart inspire us with the same feelings and thoughts which strengthen You, in obedience to the Father, to suffer humiliation and death on the cross. Oh Heart of Jesus, bless us so that our sorrows may serve as means to chasten us and detach us from the pleasures of this world. Oh Sweet Jesus, on the cross, You forgave us our sins and through the sacrament of penance, You forgive us when we sin. Through Your perfect example of love and forgiveness, grant us Your healing so that our crosses may not lead us to bitterness and hatred but rather to sweetness, joy and peace.

Fifth Day

Oh Sweet Jesus, in our most difficult moments, Your Heart is our safest refuge. Our most difficult moments will be the end of our lives when we face the just judgment of God. As God is infinitely good, we can never do enough to appease Him for our offenses against Him. So, Heart of Jesus, Be our safe refuge at the terrible moments of God's judgments at the hour of our deaths. Heart of Jesus, we pray for all souls to sincerely repent of their sins before their death and prepare themselves to be in the state to take refuge in Your heart as the truest preparation for death. Oh Sacred Heart of Jesus, we place all our trust in You.

Sixth Day

Oh Heart of Jesus, bless all persons in whatever occupations they are engaged in, at workplaces, entertainment, sports and social functions. May the Heart of Jesus be present even when we seek our material interest so that infused with the gifts of the spirit, we may use them for God's purpose for the good of others and help us on the road to salvation. May God keep away from us material things that may ruin our eternal salvation and give us only what will promote our eternal good and may we learn to hold in contempt, passing fortunes and pleasures that lead to damnation.
Oh Sacred Heart of Jesus, protect and watch over our harmful desires.

Seventh Day

Oh Heart of Jesus, Your gifts are constantly pouring out on all who have the heart to receive these gifts. Infused in our hearts the desire to receive the gifts pouring from Your Heart but as we cannot receive supernatural things without giving ourselves time for reflection, we pray for the gift of recollection so that we may have time to think of the shortness of our lives and how we should use our short lives to prepare for our salvation and that of the whole world. We invoke God's mercy to give us the gifts through Your Heart so that all mankind will have time for reflection on the things they have done that darken the soul and prevent them from receiving the gifts of God's spirit. Oh Sacred Heart of Jesus, rescue us from our wretchedness so that we may have time to think of our true end which is in God.

Eighth Day

Oh Heart of Jesus, You are our safe refuge but we live in various forms of misery because we have not trusted in Your mercy flowing from Your Heart. We have put ourselves in our various forms of misery because we have yielded to the whispering of the Devil who convinces us that nothing can be done about our spiritual states in which we find ourselves. Many refuse to know or think about their state of spiritual misery. They refuse to think of purgatory or hell because they have lost grip of supernatural things in the mystery of redemption. Others go to confessions without any real intention to remove themselves from the repeat sins which they commit. Others also receive the Holy Communion without any reverence towards what is truly the Body of Christ Himself. All these miserable persons live in a state of coldness, ingratitude and contempt.

Oh Sacred Heart of Jesus, from the graces pouring from Your Heart, transform us into new persons. Give us the courage and determination through prayer and sacrifice to remove all the obstacles to our perfection so that through devotion to Your Heart, our hearts may be united to Your Heart, to love holiness that will make us the true children of God.

Ninth Day

Oh Heart of Jesus, we thank You for the gifts that we have received from Your Heart by faithfully praying to Your Heart during this novena. We have prayed the novena united in spirit to the assembly of God's people, the Body of Christ. May Your Heart reign in the hearts of all the people of God, our Holy Father the Pope, the hierarchy of the Church, priests and religious. May the Heart of Jesus protect the faithful consecrated to God's service so that they may be true and faithful witnesses to the Gospel and make sacrifices for the salvation of souls. May they lead the faithful in the devotion to the Heart of Jesus, the source of all the gifts necessary for salvation. May they believe and practice true devotion to the Heart of Jesus and may they know that the greatest works of God can only be accomplished through the Heart of Jesus.

Oh Sacred Heart of Jesus, we place all our trust in You. May your kingdom come.

Act of Consecration to the Sacred Heart of Our Lord Jesus Christ
O Lord Jesus, holy and sweet love of our souls who has promised that wherever two or three are gathered together in Your name, You will be there in their midst, behold, O Divine and most amiable Jesus, our hearts united in one common accord to adore, praise, love, bless and please Your most Holy and Sacred Heart, to which we dedicate ourselves and consecrate our hearts for time and eternity. We renounce forever all love and affection which are not in the love and affection of Your adorable Heart; we desire that all the desires, longings and aspirations of our hearts may be always according to the good pleasure of Your Heart, which we wish to please as much as we are able. But as we can do nothing good of ourselves, we beg You, O most adorable Jesus, by the infinite goodness and meekness of Your most Sacred Heart, to sustain our hearts and confirm them in the resolution of loving and serving You, with which You inspire them in order that nothing may ever separate us or disunite us from You, but that we may be always faithful and constant in this resolution. We sacrifice to the love of Your Sacred Heart all that can give vain pleasure to our hearts and all that can engross them uselessly with the things of this world where we confess that everything besides loving

and serving You alone is vanity and affliction of spirit. O Divine and most amiable Lord and Saviour Jesus Christ, may You be blessed, loved and glorified eternally. Amen.

Act of Reparation to the Sacred Heart of Jesus

O Divine Heart of Jesus, inexhaustible Source of love and goodness, ah! How I regret that I have forgotten You so much and loved You so little. O Sacred Heart, You merit the reverence and love of all hearts which You have cherished so much and laid under infinite obligations. And yet You receive from the greater number nothing but ingratitude and coldness, and especially from my own heart which merits Your just indignation. But Your Heart is all full of goodness and mercy, and of this I wish to avail myself to obtain reconciliation and pardon. O Divine Heart, I grieve intensely when I see myself guilty of such cowardice and when I consider the ungrateful conduct of my wicked heart, which has so unjustly stolen the love that it owes to You and bestowed it on myself or on vain amusements.

O Heart most meek, if the sorrow and shame of a heart that recognizes its error can satisfy You, pardon this heart of mine for it is sorry for its infidelity and ashamed of the little care which it has taken to please You by its love. O Sacred Heart of my Saviour, what could I expect from all this but Your displeasure and condign punishment if I did not hope in Your mercy. O, Heart of my God, Heart most holy, Heart to which alone belongs to pardon sinners, do You in Your mercy pardon this poor miserable heart of mine. All its powers unite in a supreme effort to make reparation to You for its wanderings from You and the disordered application of its love.
Ah! How have I been able to refuse You my heart, I who have so many obligations to make You its sole possessor, nevertheless I have done so. But now how I regret that I have wandered away from You, from the love of You who are the Source of all goodness, in a word, from the Heart of my Jesus, who although needing me not, has sought me out and lavished Your favours on me. O adorable Heart of Jesus, is it possible that my heart can have treated You thus,

my heart which depends entirely on Your love and Your benefits and which, if You should take them from it, would fall into the utmost extremes of misery or be reduced to nothingness? Ah! How I am beholden to Your goodness, O indulgent Heart of my Saviour, for having borne with me so long in my ingratitude! Oh! How timely Your mercies come to pardon my poor, inconstant heart!

O Heart of my Jesus, I now consecrate to You and give You all my love and the source of my love, which is my heart; I give You both irrevocably, although with great confusion for having so long refused You your own possessions. O Divine Heart, my very capability of bestowing my poor heart on You is a proof of Your great love for me, but alas! I have availed myself badly of such a favourable opportunity to merit Your love and grace. Oh! How great is my confusion at the thought of this! O Heart of my Jesus, reform my faithless heart, grant that, going forward, it may bind itself to Your love by its own, and that it may approach You as much in the future as it has wandered away from You in the past, and as You are the Creator of my heart, may You, I beg You, one day give it the crown of immortality.

Litany of the Sacred Heart of Jesus
Lord, have mercy on us.
Christ, have mercy on us.
Lord, have mercy on us.
Christ, hear us.
Christ, graciously hear us.
God the Father of heaven,
God the Son, Redeemer of the world,
God the Holy Ghost,
Holy Trinity, one God,
Heart of Jesus,
Heart of Jesus, formed in the womb of a virgin mother,
Heart of Jesus united to the Word of God,
Heart of Jesus, sanctuary of the Divinity,

Heart of Jesus, temple of the Holy Trinity,
Heart of Jesus, temple of holiness,
Heart of Jesus, fountain of all graces,
Heart of Jesus, full of sweetness and humility,
Heart of Jesus, furnace of love,
Heart of Jesus, source of contrition,
Heart of Jesus, treasure of wisdom,
Heart of Jesus, ocean of goodness,
Heart of Jesus, throne of mercy,
Heart of Jesus, model of all virtues,
Heart of Jesus, house of God and gate of heaven,
Heart of Jesus, inexhaustible treasure,
Heart of Jesus, of whose fulness we have all received,
Heart of Jesus, full of mercy to those who invoke You,
Heart of Jesus, our peace and our atonement,
Heart of Jesus, living sacrifice, holy and agreeable to God,
Heart of Jesus, atoning for our sins,
Heart of Jesus, fountain of water, springing up into everlasting life,
Heart of Jesus, spring of living water,
Heart of Jesus, sorrowful in the garden, even unto death,
Heart of Jesus, weakened by a sweat of blood, Humiliated for our sake,
Heart of Jesus, filled with sorrow for our sins,
Heart of Jesus, made obedient, even to the death of the cross,
Heart of Jesus, pierced by a spear,
Heart of Jesus, exhausted of Your blood on the cross,
Heart of Jesus, refuge of sinners,
Heart of Jesus, strength of the just,
Heart of Jesus, consolation of the afflicted,
Heart of Jesus, support of those who are tempted,

Heart of Jesus, terror of the evil spirits,

Heart of Jesus, perseverance of the just,

Heart of Jesus, hope of the dying,

Heart of Jesus, joy of the saints,

Heart of Jesus, king and centre of all hearts,

From all sin, Lord Jesus, deliver us.

From hardness of heart, Lord Jesus, deliver us.

From everlasting death, Lord Jesus, deliver us.

Lamb of God, who takest away the sins of the world: spare us, O Jesus.

Lamb of God, who takest away the sins of the world: graciously hear us, O Jesus.

Lamb of God, who takest away the sins of the world: graciously hear us, O Jesus.

Lamb of God who takest away the sins of the world: have mercy on us, O Jesus.

Jesus, hear us.

Jesus, graciously hear us.

First Saturday Devotion

Meditation and Prayers in the Company of the Blessed Virgin Mary: opening prayers

Almighty and everlasting God, Creator of Heaven and Earth, You created us in holiness and love for Yourself only. We, the people of God, have assembled here under the banner and patronage of Our Lady of Fatima to meditate with her the message which, in your merciful love, you willed that the Virgin Mother of Your Son should carry to her children on earth.

Almighty God, we remember that in the days of old, You sent Your holy prophets to warn the rebellious children of Israel whenever they strayed from Your ways. These Your holy prophets gave warnings of the consequences of sin and through punishment and penance You brought them to holiness. In our day, You have sent us the Blessed Virgin Mary, the new Eve promised of old to remind us of the dangers and darkness facing the world. She carried us this message from our true God to open our eyes to our miserable spiritual condition that we have brought on ourselves through disobedience of God's commandments and our determination to instal in our midst strongholds of spiritual and moral perversions which seek to replace God's truth. Our Holy Mother mercifully reminds us that in our pursuit of temporal affairs, we have neglected our true end which is God our Creator. She calls us to arm ourselves with the sure weapons against evil: prayer, penance, sacrifice and faithful observance of the sacraments, especially the Eucharist.

Oh Father of us all, bless this assembly of your people, deliver us from spiritual darkness and eternal death. May we come to know You by the faithful observance of Your commandments which is the surest way to peace in our families, communities and the world. On our part, we promise to start the process of true repentance, reparation for our sins and those of the whole world.

Meditation on the First Apparition of the Angel

Let us read Lucia's account of the children's first encounter with the angel:

"After having taken our lunch and said our prayers, we began to see, some distance off, above the trees that stretched away towards the east, a light, whiter than snow, in the form of a young man, transparent, and brighter than crystal pierced by the rays of the sun. As he drew nearer, we could distinguish his features more and more clearly. We were surprised, absorbed, and struck dumb with amazement."

Lucia goes on to describe how the angel knelt on the ground and bowed down until his head touched the ground and recited the following prayer: "My God, I believe, I adore, I hope and love You! I ask pardon of You for those who do not believe, do not adore, do not hope, and do not love You!"

Let us all repeat the words of the angel three times.

The angel finally implored the children to pray because the hearts of Jesus and Mary were attentive to their prayers. Let us all pray with sincere hearts deeply meditating on the hearts of Jesus and Mary which have loved us so much. (The First Mystery of the rosary)

The Second Apparition of the Angel

In the second apparition, the angel spoke as follows: "Pray! Pray very much. The Hearts of Jesus and Mary have designs of mercy on you. Offer prayers and sacrifices constantly to the most high." He explained further: "Make of everything you can a sacrifice, and offer it to God as an act of reparation for the sins by which He is offended, and in supplication for the conversion of sinners. You will thus draw down peace upon your country. I am its guardian angel, the Angel of Portugal. Above all, accept and bear with submission, the suffering which the Lord will send you." (Second decade of the rosary)

Prayer

God our Father, bless us that we may seriously reflect on your mysteries and especially to understand the value of prayers and sacrifices for our salvation and enlighten our minds so that we may know You through the observance of Your commandments. Also, through observing Your commandments, we may find joy in Your presence and love You with sincere heart. It is only by truly loving You that we can be Your true children in Christ and help in the redemption of our fellow human beings.

The Third Apparition of the Angel: meditation on the story of Lucia

Lucia described how the angel appeared holding a chalice in his hands with a host above it and that drops of blood were falling into the chalice. She said the angel left the chalice and the host suspended in the air, prostrated on the ground and said the following prayer three times:

"Most Holy Trinity, Father, Son and Holy Spirit, I adore You profoundly, and I offer You the most precious Body, Blood, Soul and

Divinity of Jesus Christ, present in all the tabernacles of the world, in reparation for the outrages, sacrileges and indifference with which He Himself is offended. And through the infinite merits of His most Sacred Heart, and the Immaculate Heart of Mary, I beg of You the conversion of poor sinners." (Repeat three times)

Lucia concluded by revealing that the angel gave the Blood of Christ in the chalice to Francisco and Jacinta but gave her only the consecrated Host, saying the following prayer:

"Take and drink the Body and Blood of Jesus Christ, horribly outraged by ungrateful men. Repair their crimes and console your God." (A decade of the rosary)

Meditation on the appearance of the angel of Portugal

The role that the angel fulfilled at Fatima is not different from the part that angels have played in the sacred scripture. They were created to serve God's purposes, to adore Him and serve Him as faithful messengers and protect mankind against the forces of Satan. When Moses was crossing the desert as leader of the Israelites, God told him: "Behold, I send an angel before you, to guard you on the way and to bring you to the place which I have prepared. Give heed to him and hearken to his voice. Do not rebel against him, for he will not pardon your transgression; for my name is in him." (Exod. 23, 20-21). Also in Psalm 91, the following is stated: "Because you have made the Lord your refuge, the most high your habitation, no evil shall befall you, no scourge come near your tent. For He will give his angels charge of you to guard you in all your ways. On their hands, they will bear you up, lest you dash your foot against the stone." It is therefore not surprising that the presence of the angel had the following effect on Lucia: "The force of the presence of God was so intense that it absolved us and almost completely annihilated us." The angel therefore came to prepare the children for the arrival of the Mother of God by recalling to their minds the need for faith, love of God and the truth of our redemption through the Eucharist.

Messages of the Blessed Virgin Mary to the World from the apparitions of Fatima

First Apparition on 13th May 1917

1 Our Lady confirmed to the children that she came from heaven. To confirm this, she disclosed to the children the whereabouts of their two friends who had died: One was in purgatory and the other was in heaven.

2 Our Lady disclosed that because God wanted to use them for His purposes, they would undergo sufferings and trials but that they must accept the trials as reparation for the conversion of sinners. She assured them however that God would send them graces to strengthen them in all their trials.

3 Our Lady blessed the children, sending them graces that penetrated their souls and according to Lucia, it helped them to see themselves in God who was light making them fall on their knees, repeating in their hearts the following prayer: "Oh Most Holy Trinity, I adore You! My God, My God, I love You in the most Blessed Sacrament."

Second Apparition on 13th June 1917

1 Our Lady revealed to the children the importance of praying the rosary.

2 She entrusted to Lucia a mission that she would live long to spread the message and devotion of Fatima and like the true prophet of God, predicted the early death of the other two children Jacinta and Francisco.

3 The children could see in the palm of Our Lady's right hand, a heart encircled by thorns which pierced it. The children were made to understand that it was the Immaculate Heart of Mary outraged by the sins of humanity and seeking reparation.

Third Apparition on 13th July 1917

1 Our Lady repeated the importance of saying the rosary for

peace in the world because only she could intercede to end wars and conflicts.

2   She repeated the need for sacrifice on behalf of sinners and the saying of the following prayer whenever we make some sacrifice: "Jesus, it is for love of You, for the conversion of sinners and in reparation for the sins committed against the Immaculate Heart of Mary."

3   Our Lady opened her hands and rays of light penetrated the earth making the children have a vision of hell which came as a sea of fire. They saw the fire of hell, demons and souls in human form. Our Lady told the children "You have seen hell where the souls of poor sinners go. To save them, God wishes to establish in the world devotion to my Immaculate Heart. If what I say to you is done, many souls will be saved and there will be peace in the world."

4   Our Lady requested the children that they should say after each mystery of the rosary the following prayer: "Oh my Jesus, forgive us, save us from the fire of hell. Lead all souls to heaven, especially those who are most in need."

Fourth and Fifth Apparition on 13th August 1917

1   She repeated the need for prayers and sacrifices for sinners because many souls go to hell, as there are no people sacrificing themselves and praying for them.

Sixth Apparition on 13th September 1917

1   She repeated the need to pray the rosary for peace in the world and like God's prophet, disclosed that she would appear the following month with Saint Joseph and the Child Jesus to bless the world and that God was pleased with the sacrifices of the children.

Seventh Apparition on 13th October 1917

1   The prophecy was fulfilled when Saint Joseph appeared with the Child Jesus and Our Lady, robed in white with

a blue mantle. Saint Joseph and the Child Jesus blessed the world, tracing the sign of the cross with their hands.

2   Our Lord also appeared with Our Lady as Our Lady of Dolours and Our Lord blessed the world.

3   Our Lady appeared alone as Our Lady of Mount Carmel holding the scapular.

Special Message to Lucia on 10th December 1925

Our Lady appeared to Lucia with the Child Jesus and said the following: "Have compassion on the Heart of Your Most Holy Mother, covered with thorns with which men pierce it at every moment, and there is no one to make an act of reparation to remove them." She was referring to people's blasphemies against her and ingratitude.

She promised to assist at the hour of death, with the graces necessary for salvation, all those who, on the first Saturday of five consecutive months shall confess, receive Holy Communion and recite five decades of the rosary with the intention of making reparations to her.

On the question of this first Saturday devotion, Lucia had an encounter with the Child Jesus on the 15th February 1926, during which Our Lord made revelations on the making of the first Saturday devotion. Our Lord requested that in order to receive the full graces that are promised by that devotion, it would please Him more if the devotions were done with fervour and with the intention of making reparation to the Immaculate Heart of Mary and not with the sole purpose of obtaining the benefits of salvation.

Act of Consecration to the Immaculate Heart of Mary

O Immaculate Heart of Mary, Queen of Heaven and Earth and tender Mother of men, in accordance with thy ardent wish made known at Fatima, I consecrate to thee myself, my brethren, my country and the whole human race. Reign over us and teach us how to make the Heart of Jesus reign and triumph in us as it has reigned and triumphed in thee.

Reign over us, dearest Mother, that we may be Thine in prosperity and in adversity; in joy and in sorrow; in health and in sickness; in life and in death. O most compassionate Heart of Mary, Queen of Virgins, watch over our minds and our hearts and preserve them from the deluge of impurity which Thou didst lament so sorrowfully at Fatima. We want to be pure like Thee. We want to atone for the many sins committed against Jesus and Thee. We want to call down upon our country and the whole world the peace of God in justice and charity.

Therefore, we now promise to imitate Thy virtues by the practice of a Christian life without regard to human respect. We resolve to receive Holy Communion on the First Saturday of every month and to offer Thee five decades of the Rosary each day together with our sacrifices in a spirit of reparation and penance. Amen.

Act of Reparation to the Immaculate Heart of Mary

Most Holy Virgin, and Our beloved Mother, we listen with grief to the complaints of Thy Immaculate Heart, surrounded with thorns which ungrateful men place therein at every moment by their blasphemies and ingratitude. Moved by the ardent desire of loving Thee as our Mother and of promoting true devotion to the Immaculate Heart, we prostrate ourselves at Thy feet to prove the sorrow we feel for the grief that men cause Thee and to atone by means of our prayers and sacrifices for the offenses with which men return Thy tender love. Obtain for them and for us the pardon of so many sins. A word from Thee will obtain grace and forgiveness for us all. Hasten O Lady, the conversion of sinners, that they may love Jesus and cease to offend God, already so much offended, and thus avoid eternal punishment. Turn Thine eyes of mercy toward us so that henceforth we may love God with all our hearts while on Earth and enjoy Him forever in Heaven. Amen.

Novena to Saint Joseph

First Day

Oh Blessed Joseph, True and Worthy Spouse of Our Blessed Mother. You were destined from all eternity to be the Spouse of the Mother of God. In this most worthy vocation, you had a special honour of being chosen by the adorable Trinity. By special divine light, you were able to perform the impossible vocation of making your home in Nazareth, a place of reconciliation between God and man, between heaven and earth. You were therefore raised to a dignity which no other preacher, either man or angel, was deemed worthy to share. I, an unworthy servant of God, therefore beg you to obtain for me, the grace to imitate your great love of purity, the strength to overcome all trials and temptations and to obtain the virtues to which your co-operation with divine grace raised you in this world.

Second Day

Oh Blessed Joseph, you were chosen by God your heavenly Father, to represent Him as Father of His Son on earth. You were given the extra-ordinary honour to exercise parental authority over Our Lord Jesus Christ. Jesus Himself was pleased to be obedient to you and was ready to undertake all labours to help you to provide for His wants and to protect Him from danger. For the sake of the humility with which you performed this exalted position, obtain for me a strong and tender love for Jesus, especially love for Him in the Holy Eucharist so that I may become one with Him as He and the Father are one. Be a Father to me too and may divine love transform me, through your intercession, into a little child in your arms.

Third Day

Oh Father Joseph, how glorious was your dignity as the Father of Jesus Christ. You were made the master of the Saviour and were given the power to do with Him as a Father would do to a child. Jesus became a sharer in all your labours and hardships; thank you for your profound respect for the adorable person of Jesus Christ and the humility with which you exercised authority over him. Through your perfect example, teach all your children how to exercise authority. May we consider all authority as given to us by God and may we exercise it according to God's will and holding all offices in place of God, we may treat our brothers and sisters with true charity, respect and kindness.

Fourth Day

Oh Holy Joseph, the Holy Spirit gave you the title of "Just", which meant that you possessed exemplary virtues. Your holiness made you worthy to be the spouse of the Mother of God and to be the foster father of His son. By the purity of your heart, you became detached from all worldly things and through obedience to God's will, you advanced in perfection. We honour and revere your extraordinary holiness which places you above all other saints. Obtain for me, Oh my dear Father and patron, the grace to worthily receive the Eucharist so that like Christ, I may show God's charity to mankind.

Fifth Day

Saint Joseph, you were a model of justice in your duties to God. Your only desire was to obey God's will perfectly. You were also a model of justice towards your neighbour, in thought, word and action. Faced with the incomprehensible mystery of the incarnation, you nevertheless showed perfect charity towards a Blessed Virgin Mary and never complained in helping to fulfil God's plan of salvation. You indeed became our divine Lord's first disciple. Teach us therefore the way to observe God's law with perfect humility and always to seek the inspiration of the Holy Spirit, to love our neighbour and to serve God in our neighbour to the utmost of our ability.

Sixth Day

Saint Joseph, you were the crown of all the patriarchs and all the ancestors of the promised Messiah. All their virtues were concentrated and perfected in your person. You were also the crown of the saints of the New Testament because as the head of the Holy Family, of which Jesus Christ was a member, you proved yourself most worthy and so surpassed all the other saints of God in glory. Pray for us therefore to imitate your lively and most fruitful works and your zeal for the honour of God and salvation of man. Elevated as you now are in heaven, forget not your poor miserable children on Earth so that one day, we shall taste of the fruits of glory with you in heaven.

Seventh Day

Oh Saint Joseph, you were especially favoured, assisted and honoured by the angels. From them you received comfort in your anguish and light and direction in times of difficulties. With their help, you were able to discharge your duty as the guardian angel of Jesus and Mary. You discharged these functions with your virtues of simplicity, innocence and fervour. We turn to you then, with an ardent desire to conform ourselves perfectly to the Divine Infant whom you protected. Obtain for us all the virtues we need for Christian living. May we be guided by the assistance of the angels and saints of God.

Eighth Day

Saint Joseph, you were the model of all those who engaged in interior recollection and through silence, retirement and prayer, are led to contemplate God's gifts to mankind and show greater love of God. But you were also a model of the active life by your care of the Holy Family. You were therefore ready to assist your neighbour in the law of God as and when necessary. Pray for us to learn recollection and care while avoiding all useless conversation and the cares of this world. May we imitate your virtues and learn to converse with God and be prepared to glorify Him eternally with you after this life.

Ninth Day

Oh Blessed Saint Joseph, even in this life, you found happiness because you saw Man-God face to face for thirty years as the foster father of Jesus. You also beheld the Holy Life and charity of Jesus Christ and imitated them perfectly. Through your intercession, help us to overcome our passions for earthly things and rather devote our minds and hearts to the contemplation of things which are spiritual and heavenly. Pray for us for a strong and lively faith, in order to become detached from all earthly things. By contemplating Jesus Christ in the Eucharist, may we do good works so that even in this life of sorrow, we may have a foretaste of the happiness which awaits us in heaven.

Litany of Saint Joseph

Lord, have mercy on us.

Christ, have mercy on us.

Lord, have mercy on us.

Christ, hear us.

Christ, graciously hear us.

God, the Father of heaven, have mercy on us.

God the Son, Redeemer of the world, have mercy on us.

God the Holy Ghost, have mercy on us.

Holy Trinity, one God, have mercy on us.

Holy Mary, spouse of Saint Joseph,

Saint Joseph, spouse of Mary, the mother of Jesus,

St Joseph, virgin spouse of a virgin mother,

Saint Joseph, guardian of the virginity of Mary,

Saint Joseph, father of the Son of God,

Saint Joseph, nurse of the Child Jesus,

Saint Joseph, organ of the Word reduced to silence,

Saint Joseph, redeemer of our Redeemer,

Saint Joseph, saviour of our Saviour,

Saint Joseph, guide of Jesus in His flight,

Saint Joseph, teacher of incarnate Wisdom,

Saint Joseph, minister of the great council,

Saint Joseph, depository of the celestial treasure,

Saint Joseph, man of consummate justice,

Saint Joseph, model of perfect obedience,

Saint Joseph, lily of spotless purity,

Saint Joseph, zealous lover of our souls,

Saint Joseph, protector of religious houses,

Saint Joseph, defender of the agonizing,

Saint Joseph, patron of those who die in the Lord,

Lamb of God, who takes away the sins of the world, spare us, O Lord.

Lamb of God, who takes away the sins of the world, hear us, O Lord.

Lamb of God, who takes away the sins of the world,
have mercy on us.
Pray for us, O Holy Saint Joseph.
That we may be made worthy of the promises of
Christ.

Let Us Pray

Be mindful of us, o Blessed Joseph! And grant us the assistance
of your protection with Him who has called you father; and also
render favourable to us the most Blessed Virgin, your spouse, and the
mother of Him, who, with the Father and the Holy Ghost, lives and
reigns for ever and ever. Amen.

Prayers in Honour of the Seven Dolours and Joys of St Joseph

Chaste spouse of the Immaculate Mother of Jesus! Glorious St.
Joseph! permit me to commemorate the mental agony which
you endured with regard to your sacred spouse; deeming yourself
under the painful necessity of leaving her, until the angel banished
your doubts, and filled you with unspeakable joy, by revealing the
mystery of the Incarnation: by your anguish and holy joy on this
occasion, obtain for me, I implore, both now and in my agony, the
joy of a good conscience, sincere charity towards all men, and the
consolation of dying with you in the embraces of Jesus and Mary.

Our Father, Hail Mary, Gloria

O thrice happy Joseph! Deeply impressed with a sense of the sweet
and sacred duties which, as a father, you were called on to render
to the "Word Incarnate", permit me to commemorate the sorrow
which filled your breast on beholding that Divine Infant lying on
straw, in a manger, weeping, shivering with cold, and enduring all
the privations of the most abject poverty. But how great was your
consolation shortly after, to hear the canticle of peace intoned by the
blessed spirits, and to witness the kings of the Earth humbly prostrate
at the Infant's feet, while their countenances beamed with love, joy

and admiration, and offering their most precious gifts to Him whom they acknowledged as heaven's King! By your anguish and holy joy on this occasion, obtain that my heart may be always a pure and holy sanctuary, where Jesus will love to dwell by His grace and His real presence in the adorable Eucharist; and that, when the trials of life and the shades of death shall have passed away, my ears may be enchanted with the harmonies of the heavenly choirs, and that I may enter into the possession of those joys that neither eye has seen, ear heard, nor the human heart conceived. Amen.

Our Father, Hail Mary, Gloria.

You were, O great Saint Joseph! a man according to God's own heart, for His Law was your meditation. Permit me to commemorate the acute sensibility of your tender heart, when by the law of circumcision, it became your painful duty to cause the first effusion of the precious blood of the innocent "Lamb". The sword which pierced His Infant flesh wounded your heart; but the sweet name of "Jesus", which, in accordance with the revelation of the angel, you did bestow on Him, imparted a holy and soothing unction to your soul. By your anguish and holy joy on this occasion, pray to your Blessed Son, that, being purified in the laver of His precious blood, and all inordinate inclinations being circumcised, I may have the sweet and saving name of Jesus always engraven on my heart, and be so happy as to invoke it with great love and efficacy at the hour of death. Amen.

Our Father, Hail Mary, Gloria.

O Faithful Saint Joseph! to whom the mysterious secrets of our redemption were confided, permit me to commemorate the sorrow which filled your afflicted heart on hearing Simeon's prophecy concerning the sufferings of Jesus and Mary. But how much were you comforted on hearing immediately after that the Child Jesus was destined for the resurrection and salvation of many! By your anguish and holy joy on this occasion, obtain for me grace to participate in the dolours of Mary, and the bitter passion of her beloved Son, that by patient suffering, and heartfelt compunction, I may one day rise to a glorious resurrection, through the merits of Jesus Christ, and the intercession of His most Blessed Mother. Amen.

Our Father, Hail Mary, Gloria.

O Zealous guardian of the Son of God, and pious comforter of His dear mother! Permit me to commemorate the trials and anxiety you underwent in their service, but especially in your flight into Egypt, and the hardships of your exile, for which, however, you were in some degree consoled, by seeing the idols fall prostrate in the presence of the only true God. By your sufferings and holy joy on this occasion, obtain for me, I beg of you, grace to destroy all the idols of self-love to which I may have erected an altar in my heart, and that, henceforth, devoting all the energies of my soul to the service of you and Mary, I may live and die as you did in union with them. Amen.

Our Father, Hail Mary, Gloria.

Angel of the Earth! Vigilant guardian of the Virgin of virgins and her blessed babe! Permit me to commemorate your painful anxiety for their safety, when, on returning home, you found the throne occupied by a tyrant no less cruel than Herod; but soon, reassured by an angel, you joyfully re-established your family in the holy house of Nazareth. By your anguish and holy joy on this occasion, obtain for me, I most earnestly implore, the great blessings of interior peace, and a pure conscience during life, and that I may die invoking the sweet names of Jesus and Mary. Amen.

Mirror of sanctity! Glorious Saint Joseph! Permit me to commemorate the affliction which you experienced on losing the Child Jesus, and the agony of your grief upon finding your search useless after the space of three days. But how inexpressible was your joy upon finding your precious treasure in the house of prayer! By your poignant anguish and ineffable joy on this occasion, obtain for me grace never to be separated from Jesus by grievous sin. And should I have the misfortune to forfeit His friendship, even partially, by venial sin, may I never suffer the day to close until I shall have made my peace with God; but especially at the hour of death, may I be closely united to Him by love, confidence, and perfect compunction. Amen.

Our Father, Hail Mary, Gloria.

Pray for us, O Holy Saint Joseph!
That we may be made worthy of the promises of Christ.

Let Us Pray
Grant, O Lord! That we may be helped by the merits of your most holy mother's spouse; and that what of ourselves we cannot obtain, may be given us through his intercession; who lives and reigns, world without end. Amen.

Chaplet of Saint Michael
Saint Michael appearing one day to Antonia d'Astonac, a most devout Servant of God, told her that he wished to be honoured by nine salutations corresponding to the nine choirs of angels, which should consist of one Our Father and three Hail Marys in honour of each of the angelic choirs.

Promises of Saint Michael
Whosoever would practise this devotion in his honour would have, when approaching the holy table, an escort of nine angels chosen from each one of the nine choirs. In addition, for the daily recital of these nine salutations he promised his continual assistance and that of all the holy angels during life, and after death deliverance from purgatory for themselves and their relations.

Method of Reciting the Chaplet
The Chaplet is begun by saying the following invocation on the medal:

O God, come to my assistance.

O Lord, make haste to help me.

Glory be to the Father, etc.

Say one Our Father and three Hail Marys after each of the following nine salutations in honour of the nine choirs of angels.

By the intercession of Saint Michael and the celestial choir of seraphim, may the Lord make us worthy to burn with the fire of perfect charity. Amen.

By the intercession of Saint Michael and the celestial choir of cherubim, may the Lord vouchsafe to grant us grace to leave the ways of wickedness to run in the paths of Christian perfection. Amen.

By the intercession of Saint Michael and the celestial choir of thrones, may the Lord infuse into our hearts a true and sincere spirit of humility. Amen.

By the intercession of Saint Michael and the celestial choir of dominion, may the Lord give us grace to govern our senses and subdue our unruly passions. Amen.

By the intercession of Saint Michael and the celestial choir of powers, may the Lord vouchsafe to protect our souls against the snare and temptations of the Devil. Amen.

By the intercession of Saint Michael and the celestial choir of virtues may the Lord preserve us from evil and suffer us not to fall into temptation. Amen.

By the intercession of Saint Michael and the celestial choir of principalities, may God fill our souls with a true spirit of obedience. Amen.

By the intercession of Saint Michael and the celestial choir of archangels, may the Lord give us perseverance in faith and in all good works, in order that we gain the glory of Paradise. Amen.

By the intercession of Saint Michael and the celestial choir of angels, may the Lord grant us to be protected by them in this mortal life and conducted hereafter to eternal glory. Amen.

Say one Our Father in honour of each of the following leading angels:

Saint Michael, Saint Gabriel, Saint Raphael, our guardian angel.

The Chaplet is concluded with the following prayers:

O Glorious Prince, Saint Michael, chief and commander of the heavenly hosts, guardian of souls, vanquisher of rebel spirits, servant in the house of the Divine King, and our admirable conductor, you who shine with excellence and superhuman virtue, vouchsafe to deliver us from all evil, who turn to you with confidence, and enable us by your gracious protection to serve God more and more faithfully every day.

Pray for us, O glorious Saint Michael, Prince of the Church of Jesus Christ.

That we may be made worthy of His Promises.

Almighty and Everlasting God, who by a prodigy of goodness and a merciful desire of the salvation of all people, have appointed the most glorious Archangel Saint Michael, Prince of Your Church, make us worthy, we beg You to be delivered from all our enemies that none of them may harass us at the hour of death, but that we may be conducted by him into the august presence of Your Divine Majesty. This we beg through the merits of Jesus Christ our Lord. Amen.

For more information, please visit www.cathlight.com